Be

IT'S NEVER TOO LATE

Ellen Curry

TRILOGY CHRISTIAN PUBLISHERS

TUSTIN, CA

Trilogy Christian Publishers

A Wholly Owned Subsidary of Trinity Broadcasting Network

2442 Michelle Drive

Tustin, CA 92780

For information, address Trilogy Christian Publishing

Rights Department, 2442 Michelle Drive, Tustin, Ca 92780.

Trilogy Christian Publishing/ TBN and colophon are trademarks of Trinity Broadcasting Network.

For information about special discounts for bulk purchases, please contact Trilogy Christian Publishing.

Manufactured in the United States of America

Trilogy Disclaimer: The views and content expressed in this book are those of the author and may not necessarily reflect the views and doctrine of Trilogy Christian Publishing or the Trinity Broadcasting Network.

Author Disclaimer: This is a work of fiction. Names, characters, places, and incidents either are the product of the author's imagination or are used fictiously, and any resemblance to actual persons, living or dead, businesses, companies, events, or locales is entirely coincidental.

10 9 8 7 6 5 4 3 2 1

Library of Congress Cataloging-in-Publication Data is available.

ISBN 978-1-64773-244-8

ISBN 978-1-64773-245-5 (ebook)

Trust in the Lord, and do good.

Dwell in the land, and feed on His faithfulness.

Delight yourself also in the Lord, and He will give you the desires of your heart.

Psalm 37:3-4 NKJV

This book is for Rose, who told me to
write the book before it's too late.

This book is for my sisters, Nancy, Patty,
and Kathleen, whose love and laughter are
the heart, soul, and inspiration for it.

And especially for my husband Dave;
without you I wouldn't be me.

Ellen

1

Ellie was four years old but felt much older that day in September 1962 when she realized she was separate from the world. Even worse, she realized the world was separate from her. She was standing on the sidewalk outside her house on the corner of Mitchell and Maple Streets in Beacon, a sleepy little town in southern Illinois. Everyone said they rolled up the streets after five o'clock, but Ellie had never seen that happen.

She looked across the street at the house with the fake-brick siding and back at her own small white house, and she shivered. Maybe with excitement. Maybe fear. Probably both. She knew for the first time that everyone—her sisters, her mom and dad, everyone else—was different and apart from her. The clear blue sky and trees, and even her red Keds sneakers, were not her, but outside of her. She stood there for a long time before going back in. Tomorrow was her first day of kindergarten, and she had to get ready.

All three of her older sisters went to school, but Ellie hadn't been allowed to go before. What really frustrated her was that they could all read, but no matter how hard she stared at her books, she couldn't figure it out. She tried to fool them into thinking she could read, but they just smiled, knowing she was only saying the words she'd memorized from the hundreds of times they'd read *Green Eggs and Ham* to her.

Ellie skipped up the concrete steps into the back door of her house, happily trying to imagine what it would be like to go to school. Her sisters brought home books and projects and friends. Ellie listened in every time she could as she played outside their rooms. She liked listening to Betsy and her friends best. Betsy would be in the eighth grade tomorrow. Her other sisters, Karen and Laura, were older, already in high school. They weren't nearly as fun as Betsy, who whispered and giggled with her friends about boys and clothes and dancing and all kinds of fun things Ellie wanted to know all about. Ellie was determined to find out everything as soon as she could.

For now, Ellie concentrated on making sure her mom understood that she had to wear her red cowgirl boots to school tomorrow. Mom had already laid out Ellie's new red plaid jumper and Mary Jane shoes. Ellie had explained to her mom that black shoes with buckles would be all wrong for her first day of school, but Mom had said, "We'll see." Ellie knew that almost always meant no, but she refused to give up. She was going to wear those red boots tomorrow, and that was that.

She heard Daddy yell from the kitchen, "C'mon girls. Suppertime!" Ellie dropped her boots on the floor and raced into the kitchen. Sunday supper always meant fried bologna sandwiches.

———

Betty Lupeny, Ellie's mom, always woke up before the rest of the family, and today she got up extra early. As she slid her small feet into house slippers and threw on her pale-green chenille robe, she yawned and ran a tired hand through her tousled brown hair. Today her baby started kindergarten, and her second oldest, Karen, started high school. Betty cringed when she also remembered that today was her first day of working as a pinky at the hospital. She couldn't imagine why she had agreed to start working again after staying home for nearly twenty years, on this of all days.

Betty had worked after high school as a telephone switchboard operator. She vividly remembered finishing her morning shift on December 7, 1941, and going home for lunch. Before she could eat her sandwich, she was startled by a frantic knocking on her door. Her co-worker Nellie had come to rush her back to work. She had answered calls on that switchboard from early afternoon until almost midnight, feeling like the whole world had crashed down around her.

But now she had to get breakfast going. Betty prided herself in cooking great meals for her family. No matter how hectic, they would have a nice breakfast this morning. She loudly slammed cupboard doors and banged pots and pans, knowing the racket would start waking her sleepy girls. By the time Ellie padded in, always first, Betty had the scrambled eggs, sliced ham, biscuits, butter, strawberry jam, milk, and orange juice on the kitchen table. Now all she had to do was get the others to the table.

Laura, the oldest sister, was already up and dressed when Betty went back to call them to breakfast. Laura had practically raised herself, learning everything by quiet observation, from tying her shoes to how to read. Laura had told Betsy and Karen to get up as she went through their room to the only bathroom, knowing that if she didn't get in there first, she'd certainly be late for school. Laura would be a junior this year. As the oldest, she had her own room at the back of the house, just off the back porch. Karen and Betsy shared the middle bedroom, and Ellie slept on a cot in Betty and Elmer's bedroom at the front of the house behind the big screened porch facing Maple Street.

As Betty came through the hallway, she heard water running in the bathroom behind the closed door. Betty shook her head when she saw Betsy still in bed with the covers pulled over her head. "Lawsy, girl, you're gonna miss your first day of school!" Betty scolded as she yanked the covers off. She tried to act angry but was secretly amused when Betsy jumped out of bed wearing her first-day-of-school clothes—a very rumpled white blouse, green plaid skirt, and white knee socks crumpled around her ankles. Betsy ran past Betty and pounded on the bathroom door, telling Laura to hurry up. "I have to go now, Karen! Let me in!"

That sent Karen into a tizzy because she had to get her hair fixed just right for her first day of high school. She would simply die if her hair wasn't perfect. She looked in the mirror one more time, brushed a few stray strands of her light brown hair into place, and sprayed Adorn hairspray lavishly over her whole head before coming out. As Karen opened the bathroom door, Betsy pushed her way in, singing, "They call her the launderess, yeah, the launderess. She washes clothes and clothes and clothes..." to the tune of "The Wanderer" at the top of her lungs. Betsy had discovered long ago that singing the wrong lyrics drove her older sisters mad.

Karen shoved Betsy, trying to get out of the door as Betsy pushed in.

Laura walked past them both, shaking her head and muttering "imbeciles" under her breath. Betty came behind Laura, shaking her finger and saying loudly, "You are driving me crazy! If you don't behave and get ready for school, I'm gonna run down the street screaming and pulling my hair!" The girls had all heard that plenty of times before, but never doubted that she was one fit away from doing exactly that.

Then Elmer came out of the bedroom, wearing only his baggy boxer shorts. He said loudly and firmly, "Enough!" Karen promptly rushed to the bedroom to finish getting ready, and Betty stomped quickly to the kitchen, out of the line of fire. Betsy soon came out of the bathroom, knowing her dad would not quietly wait for her to take her time. Her shirt was still rumpled but was now tucked in, her skirt smoothed and straightened, and her socks pulled up, but her short blond hair was still sticking up and out in all directions.

As Betsy went to the kitchen for breakfast, Ellie ran past her with red jam around her mouth, in her long blond hair, and on her hands. Ellie was a mess. Ellie ran into her sisters' bedroom, where Karen was standing in front of the mirror on the double-closet door, powdering her face. Ellie rushed in and gave Karen a big hug, getting jam all over Karen's nightgown. Karen laughed but was relieved that she hadn't decided on what to wear yet. After she hugged Ellie and told her to go wash her hands, Karen opened her side of the closet, sliding the door over Betsy's side, but she still couldn't decide between her new blue skirt and her favorite gingham dress. She decided to take off her sticky nightgown and put on her slip and bra and knee socks while she thought about the problem.

Betsy came back into the bedroom, having wolfed down a biscuit with jam, while Karen was dressing. Betsy promptly opened her side of the closet, shoving the doors over Karen's side. Betsy stood in front of her side with one hand on her hip and the other firmly keeping her side open and Karen's closed, peering in intently. Karen came back and told Betsy she needed to get in the closet. "You're already dressed! You don't even need in there. Let me in my side," she said firmly. Betsy laughed out loud in the fake laugh she knew Karen hated. The more Karen pleaded and yelled, the harder and louder Betsy laughed, keeping Karen's side of the closet shut. Finally, Ellie ran back in to show them how cute she looked in her red boots and new jumper. That distracted Betsy long enough for Karen to get back into her side of the closet.

Finally, everyone was cleaned up, fed, dressed, and ready to go. Elmer left first, wearing his best navy suit. Today, he was picking the jury for the biggest case he'd ever handled, and he was pumped for both the drama and the fight. Laura, Karen, and Betsy left next, walking several blocks to their schools. Betty and Ellie left last. Ellie's school was only five blocks from their house, but Betty wanted to walk her baby to school until she was sure she knew the way by herself. Ellie was so eager to get to school that she would have run and skipped the whole way, but Betty held her hand and made her walk like a little lady.

Also, Betty wanted to make sure Ellie looked presentable when she entered the classroom for the first day. Everyone in the family always marveled at how quickly Ellie could go from perfectly dressed with her hair combed to disheveled and grimy. Somehow, before they had even gone the five blocks to school, Betty had been horrified that Ellie's shirt was wrinkled, one knee sock had scrunched down, her pigtails were lopsided, and her jumper was askew. Betty did what she could to straighten her out before she left her, but it wasn't much use. Betty was sad that her baby was going to school and wouldn't be home with her in the mornings, and she was anxious about starting her new job in an hour.

At school, after introducing Ellie to Mrs. White, her teacher, Betty rushed home to change into her pinky outfit for work. Ellie tried to listen while Mrs. White explained all the rules, but she was entranced by all the new kids and the brightly colored letters posted all around the room, the bins with blocks and toys, the shelves with books, and the easels in the corner with all kinds of painting supplies just waiting for her to get into. Ellie was especially delighted that they would get both a snack *and* a nap!

At 601 Mitchell Street, just four blocks from the Lupenys', Suzy Radcliffe was also getting ready for her first day of kindergarten. Suzy and Ellie didn't know it yet, but they would soon be best friends. Suzy also had three sisters: a younger sister, Belle, and two older sisters, Jane and Jody. When Ellie met Suzy at school that morning, she thought Suzy had the prettiest coal-black hair she'd ever seen. It was cut in the cutest little bob with bangs. Ellie wished her pale blond hair was pretty like Suzy's.

Suzy thought it was all okay but wondered if they had any play horses and barns. The blocks and letters just didn't seem like they'd be nearly as fun as her horses. When Suzy went home at noon, she was so happy to see her mom and little Belle. She told her mom all about Mrs. White and her classmates. When she told her about Ellie, she said, "Mommy, there's a little blond Japanese girl in my class!" June realized later when she met Ellie that her little upturned eyes really did look oriental when she laughed, which she did a lot.

When Betty got home, she hurriedly changed and headed to the hospital for orientation. Ever since Elmer came home after serving as a test pilot during World War II, she had been a full-time homemaker. They had moved to Champaign, Illinois, so that Elmer could go to law school, and Betty proceeded to have three babies in four years. Time had gotten away from her, and she had just started to catch her breath in the last couple of years. Now that Ellie was in school, Betty was eager to have at least a little life of her own. She hadn't even told Elmer about her job yet, but he was so busy with his work that he barely had time to talk to her and the girls.

When Betty arrived at the orientation room with the other pinkies, she realized for the first time that she was decades older than the other five girls, none of whom looked any older than Laura. As Betty walked into the brightly lit, antiseptic office, the supervisor, Nurse Helga Von Fassen, eyed her with open derision. Betty was almost forty years old, but she was slender and buxom, not movie-star gorgeous but a real knockout for a small town like Beacon. Nurse Helga had never been married. She was tall, with a thick waist, thick ankles, and even thicker eyebrows. She lumbered and wheezed as she commanded her troops. She kept her little army of nurses and pinkies strictly in line and was always on the lookout for sass and disobedience. She took one look at Betty and decided she would be big trouble with her petite, hourglass figure and smiling, but all-too-knowing eyes. Nurse Helga made up her mind to squelch this problem before it got out of hand.

Nurse Helga ordered the pinkies to line up in front of her desk. She walked down the line as stiff and imposing as General Patton, inspecting their hair and uniforms. Finding nothing out of place on Betty, she tore into the nineteen-year-old girl next in line. "You are a disgrace! Your pin is on the wrong side. Your hair is hanging down your back. You were told to put it up in a neat bun like mine. Your shoes are all wrong! No heels in this hospital, ever!" she screeched, growing louder and more vicious every second.

The girl stammered, trying to explain, but Nurse Helga wouldn't let her get a word in edgewise. She kept berating her until Betty spoke up, interrupting her. "Today is just orientation. Can't she make those changes tomorrow?" Nurse Helga glared at Betty and snapped, "That's enough out of you, Miss High and Mighty!"

Betty snapped back, "My name is Betty Lupeny, and I don't need this crap!" She took off her pinky hat and threw it on the floor, along with her hope of ever having a career of her own. She walked out of the office, her back straight, her head high, but shaking with anger and embarrassment.

When Betty stormed out of Nurse Helga's office, she ran into Dr. Bill Finney, a friend and poker-playing buddy of Elmer's. In fact, Doc had come over to their house the Saturday before to drink beer with Elmer after they rode horses that morning. Betty didn't know Doc well herself, but she knew he was kind and that he understood much more about people than he let on. He always seemed to look right through you, as if he knew every thought in your head. She found that both irritating and intriguing.

Just as Betty stormed out of the horrible woman's office, she ran smack-dab into Doc, knocking his glasses sideways and his papers out of his hands onto the floor. Of course, this happened right in front of the nurses' station. Betty scrambled to help Doc with his papers, and Nurse Helga came out of her office, clucking her tongue at them. She said, so everyone could hear, "You'd never have made it as a pinky—or anything else. I'm glad you decided to quit before I had to bother with firing you!" This made Betty's face turn beet-red. She wanted to crawl under a rug and hide. Instead, she stood up, straightened her pink uniform dress, and said, "At least I'm not a sour, old hag like you!" Betty then turned toward Doc, apologized for running into him, and walked quickly, but with her head held high, to the elevator.

Doc got onto the elevator with her just before the doors closed. Betty burst into tears, then was horrified as she realized she was crying in front of Doc. She started cussing under her breath, a special talent she'd perfected during her marriage to Elmer. Doc acted as if he wasn't paying any attention to her at all, but he couldn't help but admire her spunk—and how well she filled out her uniform.

When they reached the first floor, Betty said, "So long" to Doc and headed out to the parking lot as fast as she could, hoping to put the whole debacle behind her. But then she realized that Doc was walking out of the hospital with her. She walked faster, hoping he would go away, but he kept walking right beside her. That infuriated her, causing her to start crying and cussing again. When she got to her car, he was still there, not saying anything but just looking at her with a small smile and bright twinkle in his eyes. As she fumbled in her handbag for her car key, she looked up and said, "What are you looking at?!" He shook his head and laughed. "I've been waiting for someone to stand up to that bully for years. I want you to know how much I appreciate getting to see that today. Well done, Betty."

That set her off crying again, further sealing her total humiliation. She finally found her key, but she couldn't get the door opened, so he took the key from her, opened the car door, and helped her get in the car. He gave her the key back, winked, and said "It'll be okay," before shutting the door. He stood back so she could drive away but stayed in the parking lot watching her as she left.

On the third floor, two nurses who'd seen everything that had happened in Nurse Helga's office watched out the window as Betty and Doc walked to her car. They couldn't wait to start the rumors flying.

After Betty got home, she had more than an hour before she had to leave to walk Ellie home from school. She got out of the wretched uniform and put on her favorite slacks and sweater. She intended to get right to work. Although still just a homemaker, Betty took great pride in caring for her home and family, but she wished someone else appreciated her hard work.

She fixed herself a glass of iced coffee and lit a cigarette. She stared out the window but didn't see the quiet street or modest homes. She thought about Doc. He was a large, burly man, always a little rumpled, never seeming to be in a hurry, always watching everything intently, as if greatly amused by it all. That infuriating, crooked smile! Oh, how embarrassing to have him witness all that! Still, she couldn't help but feel a thrill in knowing he was on her side. "Well, that's neither here nor there," she said to herself. She put Sinatra on the record player and danced for a bit before starting her chores.

As always, by five o'clock in the evening, Betty had supper on the table: pork chops, fried apples, scalloped potatoes, green beans, and a little side salad for each of them on a separate plate—a lettuce leaf with a pineapple ring and a scoop of cottage cheese with a sprinkle of paprika to make it look pretty. Just like Betty had seen in a magazine. The girls all came to the table and took their places, waiting to find out whether their dad would be home for supper. Every evening, they all waited, almost holding their breath and barely talking, waiting to find out what kind of mood he'd be in.

2

Earlier that afternoon, Elmer walked across the Beacon square from the courthouse to his office. The square was the heart of life in Beacon. All the small town's most important businesses and offices were situated on one of the four outer sides of the square, with the four main streets leading cars and trucks in and out. The Benjamin County courthouse, a brick, three-story monolith, held center stage, with parking around the outside of the building as well as around the outer ring of businesses. As Elmer made his way through the traffic, he had to watch for cars backing out from the inner spots, traffic coming onto and going off the square from all four corners, and cars backing out from the outside spots. Although most of the traffic moved slowly, the chaos of movement in so many directions made Elmer's several trips across the square every day a real challenge. Locals always knew who the out-of-towners were because they stopped at the entrance to the square with blinkers flashing, waiting for someone to give them the right-of-way, which never happened. They would eventually give up and ease out into flow, hoping not to get hit, and even more, hoping to get the heck out of there and never have to come back.

As Elmer approached his office, he wasn't thinking about the traffic. He had been born and raised in Beacon; the chaos of the square was normal to him. Elmer was busy planning his next day in court. He'd picked what he hoped to be a great jury to acquit his client of trying to hire someone to kill his wife. Elmer loved—couldn't get enough of—the fight, and this one was going to be a doozy. As usual, his archenemy, Joe Harley, the state's attorney, was his adversary. Elmer's client, a longtime, well-known, previously respected preacher, the Reverend Floyd Blomer, of the First United Gospel Church (unaffiliated), had gone on home. Elmer would meet with him tomorrow before court. For now, Elmer had to make sure that he was prepared for battle tomorrow.

Elmer was dressed in his next-to-best suit, and anyone could tell he was a lawyer, or at least someone who was confident of his authority, but he was on the short side, only about five and a half feet tall, with a stocky build, thick neck, and a full head of thick brown hair that stood up straight on top of his square head. He had piercing, intelligent blue eyes and a quick wit. He'd come up through the Depression, raised by hardworking but poor parents. When he was a kid, he had vowed to make a name for himself, and he'd done just that.

He opened the door to the wooden stairway leading to his and a few other offices on the second floor. His doorway was between the Hub and Western Auto. Beside the Hub was Battles, the best burger joint and kids' hangout ever in the history of the world.

Battles was on the southwest corner of the square. There was a sign out front, and as you walked in, on the right, there was a glass candy counter with all the kids' favorite candy bars. But the best ones were kept in a little freezer behind that counter—frozen Reese's. Next to the candy counter was a long counter in front of the waitresses' and cooks' workspace. In front of the counter were metal bar stools bolted to the floor, sporting red vinyl seats that turned all the way around. The counter and barstools took up the first three-quarters of the café. The counter in front of those stools was covered in white speckled Formica with metal strips around the edge. Beyond that were soda fountains, supplies, the griddle, and lots of signs, some printed and many handwritten. The signs extolled the virtues of Coke, the prices of the burgers and fries and sodas and candy bars, and two or three that said, "Go, Rangers!" for the high school teams. There was also one very prominent sign announcing that no cussing was allowed. On the other side were red vinyl booths going all the way to the back, where the jukebox stood. The floors were of worn wood, and the walls had been painted some nondescript color way too long ago. This was Mecca—*the* hangout for all kids from about sixth grade all the way through high school.

Willametta Battle—never called by her given name but called Willie by everyone—had come in the back door on the alley side of Battles at 6 a.m. to get ready for the day. With school starting, Willie dreaded the crush of kids who'd flood in every day like a swarm of locusts. Starting at eleven thirty in the morning, when Webster Junior High let the kids out for lunch, straight through till one fifteen in the afternoon, when the last of the high school students left, Battles would be packed with kids three deep, yelling, "Cheeseburger basket and a Coke!" and "Hot dog and a Sprite!" She and her main helpers, Billie and Bea, would flip burgers, pour soda, hand out candy, make change, break up occasional arguments, and clean up endless messes much longer than their aging bodies would go without major complaints. But Willie just shook her unruly head of curly dark-red hair and laughed. She couldn't help but love every one of the kids, pimples and all. The best times were after school, when fewer kids came in and she had time to hear them laugh and tell stories.

Willie knew that every kid who came into Battles was simply trying to figure out who he or she was and what in the heck they were supposed to do in this crazy world. Some of them confided in her, but mostly they just knew this was a safe place to come to meet their friends and have a soda or a bite to eat, where Willie and anyone else who worked there would give them an easy smile and respect. Of course, Willie didn't put up with any nonsense and quickly nipped trouble in the bud. But the kids understood her simple rules, and Willie never had any trouble that lasted or disrupted the cheerfulness of the place.

Laura and Karen had made plans to meet Betsy at Battles after school. Laura would stay after school to catch up with friends she hadn't seen over the summer. Karen was going to check in the office about becoming a student worker. Then they'd walk down East Main to the square. Since Betsy was just in eighth grade, she'd get out of school earlier. Betsy gladly agreed to wait forty-five minutes after school for them.

When Laura and Karen walked in, the place was packed, every stool taken, every booth filled. The jukebox played "Johnny Angel," and the chatter and laughter greeted their ears like a longed-for embrace. They each found their friends and stayed for as long as they could before dragging Betsy out. "You know we have to be home by four," scolded Karen. Betsy said, "Toodle-oo!" to her friends and began singing the wrong lyrics to "Duke of Earl": "He's the Kook of Pearlllll!" she sang loudly as she skipped ahead of them.

They walked past the Ben Franklin dime store, crossed West Main Street, and past the hardware store and several others to the Bank of Beacon, which wasn't technically on the square, but just off the northwest corner. They cut through the bank parking lot to North Maple Street, which ran parallel to and one block west of North Main Street, the main drag for kids riding around on the weekends. Their house was seven blocks from the square, which gave them just enough time to catch up on the most important news from each other's first day back at school. Laura was mainly happy that her friends Kathy Sue and Elaine were in her homeroom class. She also secretly hoped she'd get to see Harry Lewis at noon again tomorrow. Of course, she wouldn't breathe a word of this to her blabbermouth sisters. Harry was much older than her, already out of high school and working at a real job, so much more interesting and mature than those moronic high school boys.

Karen felt a little overwhelmed by high school—it had so many more kids than junior high, and it was so much bigger. There were three floors, with the lunchroom and lockers in the basement and wide, wooden stairs on both sides of the long, brick building between the floors. When the bell rang for class changes, hundreds of kids flooded out of the classrooms into the wide hallways and up and down the stairways. She thought the building was collapsing or that there had been an earthquake the first time she'd heard it. And finding her classes was a nightmare. She'd absolutely die if she had to walk in late in front of everyone. Thankfully, her teachers seemed nice, especially Mrs. Armentrout, her Latin teacher.

Laura assured Karen that she'd get used to the loud, boisterous high school soon, especially now that she'd be an office helper two days a week, going to classrooms before school and during her study hall to deliver supplies and messages. Karen liked having an official position in the school, and even though she was a little nervous about keeping up with it all, she knew she could trust the head school secretary, Irene Morlinski, to guide her through it. She was glad Laura had already been there for two years. Laura had told Karen most of what to expect. Still, Karen was glad she'd survived her first day without calling attention to herself or falling down those awful stairs.

As Betsy walked a little ahead of them, she acted like she wasn't listening to them, but really she was hanging on every word. After all, she would be going to high school next year, and she had to learn as much about it as possible. Eighth grade was fine, much better than Lincoln Grade School, but Betsy couldn't wait for high school. Dances! Ball games! Parties! Betsy intended to be a cheerleader and have lots of boyfriends.

As they walked down the familiar street, they saw the paper boy ride past, throwing everyone's copy of the *Beacon Evening News* into their yards. They knew who lived in most of the houses they passed, and lots of their friends lived on the side streets just blocks away. A couple of blocks before home, they saw Kennedy, the lumbering old Bassett hound that belonged to the George family, crossing the street. Kennedy liked to roam, and he was never in a hurry. It was very common when driving down Maple Street to have to stop to wait for him to make his way across. Another block closer to home, they saw Mrs. Booten pulling into the driveway of her tidy little blue house with bright white trim. They all waved and said hello to their former first-grade teacher, a sweet, short, dark-haired, slightly round lady who had taught them all.

3

Elmer went into his office at the end of the long hallway, just past two other attorneys' offices on his side. Just across the hallway from his office was the extrawide doorway leading to the huge office suite of Jessie Lupeny Jenkins, Esquire. Jessie was his aunt, his father's younger sister and the bane of Elmer's existence. He could only hope that she'd be out of town until after he left at the end of the day. No one grated on his nerves like Aunt Jessie. Elmer set his large leather briefcase in the chair next to Marge's desk. Marge was his secretary, his friend, and the most valuable asset in Elmer's office. Although he was ridiculously confident, Elmer knew full well who actually kept his business running. He greeted Marge and checked on who'd called and stopped by while he was at court.

Two minutes into the discussion, Elmer heard the thundering footsteps of the six-foot-two, 310-pound Amazon, and he visibly cringed. Now he'd have to talk to her. She'd followed his murder-for-hire case from the beginning and knew he'd begun picking the jury today. He and Marge exchanged knowing looks as Jessie barreled down the hall, Elmer like a child pleading to his mother to make the monster under the bed go away and Marge with her typical raised eyebrow and wry smile.

The door to Elmer's office flew open, and Jessie filled the doorway, wearing a giant pair of clunky, black-patent leather heels and a macabre chartreuse skirt and jacket with a hot pink blouse sporting a giant bow at the neck. On her head, she wore one of her signature billed hats with a pheasant feather stuck on the side, from under which spewed an enormous head of coal-black hair teased mercilessly into a frightful "hairdo." Two large, shiny pink balls dangled and clacked under each ear, and her makeup was one degree below clown quality. Just looking at her made Elmer's head hurt. Then she opened her mouth.

Booming, Jessie's voice could always be heard from anywhere in the building, all the way to the stairway at the front of the building, unless she was in her inner office, specially equipped with soundproof walls, ceiling, and floor. Jessie was fifteen years older than Elmer, so she was no spring chicken, but she had more energy and stamina than a team of mules. Of course, she was far more stubborn than any mule, but also smarter than anyone knew, even her courtroom opponents, whom she regularly terrified and humiliated.

"So! How'd it go, Elmer Pie?" Elmer cringed and told her for the thousandth time not to call him that. She ignored him again. "Get a decent jury for that dipwad client of yours?" Before Elmer could answer, Jessie launched into a diatribe about men who didn't treat their wives with respect. That was her worst pet peeve, having gotten married to a womanizer when she was twenty-two. They'd only stayed married four months because Jessie had caught the cheating lowlife with some floozy. Her heart was shattered. Not only did she know she'd never find another man brave enough to marry a giant like her, but she was appalled that she had actually, unconditionally, and infinitely loved a man who was too stupid to have a single intelligent conversation with her. Oh well. She always sighed when she remembered him, but she resolutely carried on with her life. No one was going to sink her.

After a quick divorce, she waited tables at night for three years while putting herself through law school. She graduated at the top of her class, but not a single law firm offered her a job, not even when she offered to work for half-pay. After a few months of begging for a job in central Illinois, she packed her bags and headed to southern Illinois, where her brother, Fred, lived. Fred worked in the coal mines, and southern Illinois wasn't any better off than the rest of the country in 1932, but Jessie knew that she could stay with Fred's family until she got her practice up and running. Thankfully for everyone, it only took her about six months to scrape together enough money from waiting tables at two restaurants to rent an office and get her own place.

While Jessie was living with Fred, she'd gotten to know and love his family. Fred's wife, Annie, was as short as Jessie was tall. But the twinkle in her eyes drew everyone to her. You just couldn't help but laugh a little easier and come closer to peace around Annie. That's not to say that Annie didn't have a temper because—look out—if you messed with her boys or if she caught Fred drinking, you'd think all hell had been unleashed.

Not long after Jessie moved in, the old plumbing to the bathroom started acting up again. Between shifts at the mine, Fred took his box of tools into the crawl space under the house to fix the problem. He worked diligently for over a week, each day coming back in the house cussing under his breath and saying he'd have to go get another part. One day Jessie got off work earlier than expected and walked by the side of the house where Fred was.

When Jessie went inside, she told Annie that Fred needed something to drink, so Annie fixed him a glass of cold lemonade and took it out to him. Before she got there, and certainly before he knew she was there, Annie saw Fred lying on his back, hammer in one hand and a bottle of beer in the other. Annie stopped to watch him. He'd take a long swig of beer, then hit the pipes a few times to make it sound like he was working. Well, Annie ran at him like a whirlwind and threw that lemonade right in his face. Before he knew what had happened, Annie had drug him by his overall straps out from under the house, scolding him for all the neighbors to hear. Fred knew the jig was up; he hung his head and went inside. Jessie then made herself scarce, a considerable task given her excessive girth and the tight quarters of Fred's two-bedroom house.

When Jessie moved out a couple of months later, she took a room at the Drake Hotel on East Main Street, next to the railroad tracks. Jessie was waiting tables at the restaurant there, so they'd let her have a small room for practically nothing. The hotel's business would have dried up completely during the Depression were it not for the railroad crews staying there every other week. Occasionally, lawyers from out of town stayed there when working on big cases at the federal courthouse on West Main Street. Jessie planned to capitalize on both groups as she tried to build a business as a female lawyer in the rigid old boys' club of the legal world. Jessie was as honest with herself as with everyone else. She knew she couldn't win anyone over with her looks. In fact, she knew most people thought she was hideous, an ogre of a woman. And she didn't have an ounce of tact. She'd never sugar-coated anything before, and she wasn't about to start now.

As the youngest of three boys, Elmer was the only one available to help Jessie move that summer. She didn't have much, but it was more than she could carry herself. Elmer, a scrawny twelve-year-old, carried one bag and a quilt Annie had made for Jessie, and Jessie carried her few law books in one bag and the rest of her clothes in another. They only had about twelve blocks to walk across town, and Jessie wanted to make the most of this opportunity with her favorite nephew. Elmer's older brothers were already out of school and working, and Jessie rarely saw them. But she'd grown very fond of this cocky, witty kid. She saw that he was smart enough to always get his way, and she was determined that his mischievousness would not lead him down a path with no future.

"So, Elmer, what are you going to do with your life?" He looked up at her and grinned from ear to ear. "Anything and everything. I'm gonna join the navy and sail around the world and eat at fancy restaurants and dance with all the prettiest girls. I'm gonna be a detective and solve crimes and write book and fly planes. Why?"

Jessie said, "I sure hope you do, Elmer. But what about a family? Don't you want to get married and have kids?"

"Well sure," he replied, "but I'm gonna do all the things I want to do before I get saddled with a wife and a bunch of bratty kids."

When they got to the hotel, Elmer exclaimed, "Whooee! I can't wait to see the inside of this place!" Although the Drake Hotel was only a small building, its exterior was quite grand for a little town like Beacon. A poor kid like Elmer could only dream about entering such a fancy establishment. As they walked across the lobby's plush red carpet and up three flights of stairs to Jessie's small room, Elmer felt out of place and embarrassed by his dirty, bare feet and ragged overalls. He promised himself that someday he'd be able to stay at the finest hotels and eat at the most elegant restaurants. He knew he would do whatever it took to be a man no one could rightfully look down on.

As they climbed the stairs, Elmer continued, "Everyone has a family. I want to be somebody, have adventures, go places. I'm not just gonna go down in that dirty mine and slave for someone else my whole life. I'm gonna start in high school, being the class president all four years and being in every play and playing football and tennis. I'm gonna be the editor of the Echo, and I'm gonna take the prettiest girls to all the dances. No one is going to stop me from living my dream."

"No one but yourself," Jessie replied.

Elmer snorted and shook his head. "I know what I'm gonna do. And I don't need anyone's help."

"Okay, whatever you say, Elmer Pie," Jessie said as she turned the key and opened the door to her room.

"Dang it, Aunt Jessie, you've got to stop calling me that. It makes me sound like a little kid. You know I'm already twelve. Dad started working in the mines when he was only nine, and both my brothers were already working by my age," Elmer complained.

"Yeah, that's sure the truth." Jessie sighed loudly, and as they put her bags on the small bed, she finally said, "Every man you know began working early and never stopped to take a breath or go anywhere or see anything till the day they died. That's not the life for you. But just remember one thing. It's never too late to be who you might have been."

"Oh, there you go again, talking nonsense that no one can understand. Thank God we're finally here." As soon as Elmer put her bag and quilt down, he was out the door and off to find his pals.

As Jessie put away her few belongings, she remembered her childhood. Hunger and cold had often made her miserable, but she barely remembered either. Instead, she remembered lots of laughter and music. She could still feel the dirt under her bare feet as she ran in the fields with her brothers, and she could smell the black earth and vegetables from their huge garden. She saw herself climbing over the wood-slatted fence into the hog pen as she brought them their slop, talking to each one because she loved them, even though they were likely to soon end up on their dinner table. She had read every book she could get her hands on. She had loved her life because her family had loved her. Everything had been so simple and meager. So pure. Then she started growing. And she kept growing until she was much bigger than her oldestbrothers, Ike and Harry.

By the time she was twelve, she was the biggest kid, boy or girl, at her school. In fact, she'd never met anyone else as big as her. At over six feet tall, she stood out like a sore thumb, heads taller than most people. Of course, the other kids were mercilessly cruel, calling her terrible names and mocking her behind her back. They would never say anything in front of her older brothers, though, for fear they would beat them black and blue. She only had one real friend outside of her family, Daisy, who lived on the farm down the road from her.

Jessie couldn't remember life before Daisy was her friend. Almost every day when they were big enough to hike the mile between their farms, they had found time to spend together. They always read each other's books and then acted out their favorite scenes for days afterward. But Daisy had died on June 30, 1925, just after Jessie finished high school. Losing Daisy was the worst thing Jessie had ever faced. Nothing else would ever come close, not even discovering that her loser husband had cheated on her. The grief had almost killed her. But it didn't. Instead, she carried it with her everywhere, every day, not as bitterness, but as a reason to look at everyone she saw with an extra measure of love. Jessie knew that everyone had a little or big piece of that heartache themselves. She couldn't help but recognize it in most people, especially the most hateful and difficult.

Besides, Jessie was naturally optimistic. What almost no one else knew, except Annie now and Daisy back then, was that Jessie prayed all the time. She wasn't afraid or embarrassed to talk about her faith, but most people just didn't get it. So, she usually didn't talk about it. She just prayed, and she read her Bible every day. Not because she had to. Only because when she did, God showed up to delight and amaze her. Jessie didn't know how other folks got through a single day without talking to God or reading His book. She knew that most people could never get beyond how she looked, how loudly she talked, and how opinionated and aggressive and driven she was. She knew that in the world, she was a freak. But, inside, she was almost always filled with joy so unspeakable that it often made her laugh out loud, which, of course, didn't help at all with that whole "freak" thing.

As Laura, Karen and Betsy walked home, Ellie sat on the front steps waiting for them. She was about to burst, wanting to tell them all about her first day of school. She thought about her friend Suzy and her teacher, Mrs. White. All those paints and easels with new paper and books for tracing out her letters and her brand-new box of crayons. She was so excited she couldn't sit still, so she jumped off the steps to the sidewalk and skipped down to the corner to look for them again. There they were! Walking toward her, talking to each other, and not paying a bit of attention to her. She started to run toward them, but then she remembered that she shouldn't go across the street by herself. She'd done that once. She wouldn't ever again...

Ellie yelled and waved and jumped up and down. "Hey, sissies! Just wait till you hear about my school!" Betsy, who was walking in front of the others, saw her first and wanted to be upset with the little brat, but she found herself walking faster to get home and see the little imp. Betsy was always torn between tormenting Ellie and making up a new game to play with her.

Laura and Karen saw Ellie and looked at each other, shaking their heads and laughing. Before school, Ellie had been dressed perfectly in her crisply ironed white blouse and new red plaid jumper. Mom had relented and allowed Ellie to wear her beloved red cowgirl boots, cringing at how scuffed and worn-out they looked. But Ellie had pleaded so desperately to wear them and had been so brokenhearted at having to wear her new shoes that Mom had given in (as usual) and let Ellie have her way.

Now Ellie still had on the red boots, but she had changed into her Indian outfit, complete with feathered headband and bow and arrow. As Ellie chattered nonstop about all the wonders of kindergarten, her sisters each hugged her and said, "Wow!" and "That's wonderful!" over her comments. Ellie soaked up their presence. She couldn't wait until she could be grown-up, just like them.

4

Back at Elmer's office, after Jessie had grilled Elmer for several more minutes, she left to go back to her office. Elmer sighed loudly and headed into his inner office to get ready for his opening statement the next day. He loved everything about jury trials—except losing, of course. Thankfully, he hadn't experienced much of that. Now that he had picked the jury, he would go over his notes about each juror, he'd review the evidence, and he'd decide how best to draw the jury into his theory of the case. Elmer knew that jury trials were far more about personalities and storytelling than facts and law. He knew the law, and he had great respect for the American jury trial system. But he knew that the personality of each juror and his (or the occasional her) background and prejudices were really in charge of the outcome. He just had to find the right key to unlock that door to victory—in this case, acquittal of a true slimeball.

As Elmer looked over his notes, he paced around his small office, seemingly talking to himself, but actually addressing tomorrow's jury. He had no window, and piles of papers and files were stacked all over the room. His framed law school diploma and practice licenses were on the wall behind his desk, but on the other three walls, he had placed framed line drawings of courtroom scenes—caricatures of the daily life of a practicing attorney: arguing to the jury, pouring over stacks of huge law books, intently interviewing an old woman. He loved those drawings and wished he'd drawn them himself. He also had placed lots of mementos around the room from his time spent oversees while in the military. They reminded him that the world was much bigger than little Beacon, and that, someday, he would see it all.

Although Elmer had been fairly successful in his practice, he could never seem to get ahead of all the bills. Raising four daughters and paying his office overhead and Marge's salary took every ounce of Elmer's energy and every dime of his money. He'd never lost his travel bug, and he took Betty and the girls on trips as often as possible. But the daily grind of keeping his office afloat and the girls in style wore heavily on him. He knew he didn't connect with his family like he should, but he didn't know how to accomplish that. Being a lawyer came naturally to him, but being a husband and father of four girls constantly flummoxed him. For now, however, he was intent on his work, thinking of nothing else. Marge stuck her head in before she left to say good night, but he didn't even notice her.

———

In her office, Jessie kicked off her shoes as soon as she got in the door and said, "Whooee! Am I glad to get those blasted heels off! So, what's up, Cookie?"

Cookie sat behind a huge, L-shaped desk neatly arranged with typewriter, books, pens, and files. Prominently displayed in front of her desk was a black marble nameplate, stating:

OFFICE MANAGER
Constance MacIntyre

Jessie relied implicitly on Cookie to run her office and keep her mouth shut when she went home. Jessie had never liked calling her office helpers "secretaries," and she hated how little other attorneys paid their help and how badly they treated them. Jessie had vowed early in her career that anyone who worked in her office would be paid royally and treated even better.

Cookie, a petite, twenty-five-year-old blonde, wearing a navy-blue blazer and crisp white blouse, looked up from her typewriter and said, "I wish you'd get some reasonable shoes so you wouldn't come in here complaining every day, but since you won't listen to me, here, take these." Cookie pulled out a large shoebox from under her desk, shoved it across the huge desk toward Jessie, and went back to her typing. Jessie, puzzled, opened the box and squealed like a little girl. "Lordy, Lordy, where on earth did you find these wonderful darlings?! I love them!" Jessie exclaimed, tearing them out of the box and pulling them onto her overworked, oversized feet. She stood up and pranced heavily around the room, continuing to "oooh" and "aaah" over her new fuzzy, hot-pink house slippers. Jessie had never been able to find house shoes big enough for her, so she was always padding around in her stocking feet. Cookie loved working for Jessie, but the stench from those giant feet trapped in nylon stockings and leather shoes all day was about to put her six feet under. Cookie told Jessie, "I've got resources you don't need to worry about. You do the lawyering, and I'll take care of the rest."

Right then, Jessie's investigator, Jack Ward, walked into the office. Jack was lean and chiseled, not handsome, but intense in a way that attracted all kinds of women. No one knew exactly how old he was or where he had lived before he came to Beacon back in the late forties. He just showed up one day, walked around the square, saw Jessie coming from the courthouse, and had been working for her ever since. Jack was Jessie's eyes and ears. He interviewed all her witnesses and tracked down leads for her. He was a loner without any family Jessie had ever heard of. But nothing ever escaped his attention, so Jessie didn't pry about his past.

She had found out about the seven years he'd spent in prison in Arkansas for an armed robbery, but she had never told him that she knew. He worked full-time for her and raised horses on a few acres out in the country in his spare time. He was quiet and diligent, and he knew how to use a gun when necessary. Jessie didn't need to know any more than that.

Jack looked at Jessie's feet and said, "Talked to that taxi driver who picked up Porter on the night of that murder. He said that Porter was so drunk he could barely get in the taxi, and he dropped him off at home just after midnight. So, Porter's alibi is solid after all."

"Fantastic, Jack. What about that gal he said was with him?" asked Jessie, as she sat down in a large, maroon, leather client chair. She had insisted all the chairs be big enough for her to sit in, too. She had her impossibly huge, fuzzy slippers stuck out in front of her, turning each of them this way and that so she could admire them from different angles.

Jack said, "No gal with him in the taxi. He must have ditched her at the party before he left. I'll find her tomorrow." He turned around and walked out the door without saying good-bye. Jessie was glad she'd at least have an alibi to use in defense of her newest client, Abe Porter, who'd been charged with murdering the husband of one of his many girlfriends.

———

At home, Betty and the girls sat down to dinner without Elmer, but none of them had really expected him. Betty had explained to them long ago that their father would not be home for dinner most nights when he was working on a jury trial. They ate a lot of dinners without him. As they sat around the kitchen table, Ellie and Betsy did most of the talking, with Laura and Karen commenting now and then. Betty mostly watched, trying to listen but often drifting away to thoughts of her own. Raising four daughters was exhausting and aggravating. She tried to be loving and kind, but too often, she found herself yelling at them like her own mother had yelled at her. Oh well, she told herself, she kept a clean house and put good food on the table. That made up for a lot.

Ellie was so excited that she was finally in school, just like her big sisters. Being the youngest was hard enough, but not being in school like them just made her plain mad. She told them all about her new friend, Suzy, and her teacher and the nap mats and the toys. Laura asked her if she had learned any letters today, and Ellie replied, "No, we start that tomorrow. I bet I'll know how to read just like you by the end of the week!" Laura smiled and said with a laugh, "I bet you will too, Ellie."

After dinner, it was Karen and Betsy's turn to clean up the kitchen and wash the dishes. "Here we go," thought Betty, knowing how much easier it would be to just do it herself, but she had committed to sticking with a chore schedule this year, and she was determined to see it through, no matter how many fights there were. Karen cleared the table and scraped the dishes, putting as many scraps as possible in a pan for Tubby, their Saint Bernard, whom Elmer had brought home a year ago, much to Betty's dismay. Tubby immediately became an indispensable member of their family, to all except Betty. It was Ellie's job to take the scraps out to Tubby and to run fresh water in his bowl. She loved Tubby and did not remember life without him. She had already told him all about her day at school as soon as she got home. Now she just scratched his big head and ran back in the house. It would soon be time for the big fight!

After Betty made sure the girls had cleaned everything and the dishes had been washed, dried, and put away, she went into the living room to watch the big fight. She sat down in the easy chair on the window side of the living room. It was Betsy's turn tonight, so she took up her place at the far corner of the room, in front of the door leading to the front porch. Betsy got on her knees and waited for the bell to ring. Ellie was in the opposite corner, in front of Betty. Ellie was standing, waiting for Betty to ring the bell. *Ding! Ding!* And out they both came, wrestling with all their might, trying to get the other to the floor first. Ellie was small for her age, but almost as tall as Betsy on her knees. They tussled and struggled, each determined to win. Finally, Betty rang the bell and declared it a draw. Betsy and Ellie fell in a heap on the floor, laughing and panting. Since no one had won, Betsy and Ellie would have another round the next night. Laura and Karen were happy to let them have this particular game.

Betsy had made up lots of games for Ellie. She took the three-foot-long, rectangular, brown couch bolsters and put one on the floor, then had Ellie lie down on it. Betsy then lavishly pretended to put mustard and ketchup and relish on Ellie's back. If Betsy was feeling particularly devious, she'd tell Ellie that she was putting sauerkraut on her, too. Ellie hated sauerkraut and would squeal horribly, believing what Betsy told her, that she'd smell just like it for two days, even if she took a bath. After Betsy got the hot dog fixed up just right, she put the other "bun" on top of Ellie and called Karen and Laura, like a hawker at a ball game, "Hot dogs! Get your hot dogs right here!" Ellie would giggle, trying to stay quiet so her sisters wouldn't know it was just her and not a real hot dog.

After the big fight, Betty took Ellie to get a bath before bed. Ellie thought it horribly unfair that her sisters got to stay up later than her, but tonight she didn't fight it. She was worn out from her big day. And tomorrow, she was going to learn how to read!

While Betty was helping Ellie find her clothes for the next day and get ready for bed, the phone rang. Betsy ran to answer it. "Hello, Lupeny residence, Betsy speaking."

"Well, hello, little darlin'. You're just the gal I need to talk to. How about coming to work for me?" asked Aunt Jessie. Betsy looked puzzled and said, "Well, what do you want me to do?"

"I need someone to clean my office. Now, don't decide yet. I've talked to your dad, and he says it's okay, but you'll have to talk to your mom. If you think you can handle it, we'll work out the details later. You just think about it and let me know. Oh, and by the way, if you agree, you'll get twenty-five cents an hour," said Jessie in her most official voice.

"Okay, thank you, Aunt Jessie." Betsy hung up the phone and shook her head. She walked back to her bedroom and said to Laura and Karen, "You won't believe what Aunt Jessie just asked me."

"What now?" asked Laura, who couldn't stand her aunt's loud, crude, overly direct ways, not to mention how the house shook every time she walked in, almost always unannounced.

"She wants me to start cleaning her office."

"What? You?" asked Karen. "Are you going to?"

"Well, maybe. I want to earn some money, but I don't think I could stand being up there all by myself, or even worse, with Aunt Jessie there all the time," said Betsy.

Just then Betty came in and exclaimed, "What does that mammoth want now?"

Betty couldn't stand Aunt Jessie and had made no attempt to conceal her disgust. Betty thought it was great for women to work, but all she could see in Jessie was an overbearing, opinionated, rude woman who barged in unannounced, making Betty feel like Jessie didn't value her time and efforts to keep an orderly household.

What Betty didn't understand was that Jessie had worked so hard to make her place in a man's world that she could hardly relate to women like Betty anymore. Sure, she respected them. Heck, if life had dealt her those cards, she'd be just like Betty. But she'd had to play the cards dealt to her, and the hand she played was not usually accepted by other women in the early 1960s. The result was that, try as she might, Jessie couldn't fit into Betty's world of raising kids, keeping house, and playing cards with her lady friends every other week. Jessie knew she might as well try to fit her size-13 feet into Betty's little, size-7 stilettos.

Jessie had an ulterior motive for asking Betsy to clean her office. She almost never did anything without an ulterior motive. As a woman lawyer, she had to maximize every benefit she could. Besides getting her office cleaned for cheap, Jessie knew that Betsy had been trained from birth to never, ever say anything to anyone about her dad's business. Betsy could be trusted, even though she was not yet thirteen years old. But Jessie's real reason for having Betsy work for her was to give her a safe place to talk about her troubles. Jessie recognized how Betty's constant criticism had worn Betsy down and was about to put out her light altogether. Betty would deny it vehemently, thinking that she treated all her girls the same, with tender, loving care.

But Jessie had barged in often enough to have heard Betty railing on Betsy with a viciousness that she clearly reserved for that child alone. She might say something less than kind occasionally to the others, but she almost never let up on Betsy. Jessie had vowed to turn the tide and build up some backbone in Betsy. Jessie knew she could never convince Betty that there was any need to change her behavior, but she hoped and prayed that she'd seen the problem soon enough to do some good for that little girl. There was surely no chance her nephew would ever see this problem.

Betsy surprised herself when she told Betty that she had already agreed to clean Jessie's office. She didn't realize it until she said the words that she really did want to do this. Besides, it would make her sisters crazy that she had money of her own when they didn't. The real reason she wanted to work for Jessie, though, was simply that it would drive her mom crazy.

"You can't work for her—what about school and cheerleading? If you think you're going to get out of doing your chores here, you are sadly mistaken, little missy," said Betty, throwing daggers at Betsy with her eyes. Betsy threw back her shoulders and told her, "Dad has already agreed to it, so you can't stop me. And I'll still take care of everything here and at school, so there's no reason to be upset."

Ellie ran in and hugged Betsy, exclaiming, "Yay! You're going to work for Auntie Jessie." Ellie was Jessie's little Ellie Dellie, the only one in Elmer's family who really, truly loved Jessie. Karen was intrigued by her, and she came the closest of the others to liking her, but Ellie absolutely adored her aunt, thinking she was like a big bear who wore lots of colorful jewelry and the funnest makeup she'd ever seen.

Once, Ellie had gotten into Laura's makeup and had tried to fix herself up like Auntie Jessie. Her mom had laughed so hard she'd peed her pants a little, but Laura was crushed. She had just bought that makeup with money she had saved from her birthday and Christmas. She wanted to be really mad at Ellie, but seeing her with bright blue eyelids, bright red circles on her cheeks, and ruby-red lipstick smeared all over her lips and beyond, Laura soon started laughing, making herself even more mad. Finally, when Karen and Betsy had come in from the front porch to see what was going on, they started laughing, too. When Elmer came home a few minutes later, he looked into the bedroom at all four of them in a heap on the floor still laughing so hard they had tears streaming down their faces. Ellie was walking around in Laura's heels like Auntie Jessie and saying in as deep a voice as she could muster, "Elmer Pie, you are such a dweeb. Don't you know anything about how to treat little girls?"

Elmer cringed, turned around, and walked as fast as he could into the living room. Sometimes he was sure he had sired another species. All these females!

Before Ellie fell asleep, Karen came in to say good night. Betty had already tucked Ellie into her little cot at the end of the big bed where she and Elmer slept. Karen told Ellie how much she loved her and how very special she was. Karen was the one who fixed Ellie's long hair, and she doted on her little sister. Karen had seen how harsh Betty was with Betsy and how much it hurt Betsy. Karen couldn't figure out any way to help Betsy or to stop her mom from saying such hurtful things, but she had vowed to herself that nothing bad like that would ever happen to Ellie.

5

Jessie had gone home early that evening, at least for her. It was around 7 p.m., and she had decided to go for a long walk. She did this frequently, taking her old hound dog, Goober, as far as they could walk without collapsing, and only then turning around. She had to clear her head, and she didn't know any better way to do that than to go for a long walk with her best pal. Jessie lived in the same neighborhood as Elmer's family, but closer to the edge of town. She had found several routes to the forestry just north of town. She liked to walk there, whether it was rainy and dark or sunny and bright. She loved the sharp smell of pine needles and the soft feel of the ground under her feet. She spied birds, bugs, wildflowers, and an occasional snake. Goober gloried in all the smells, along with the rabbits and squirrels he scared up. Mostly, Jessie talked to God. And she did her best to listen when He talked to her, showing her just exactly what she needed to know at the precise moment she needed it. Jessie was wise enough to understand that she knew absolutely nothing of value on her own, but as she paid attention to God's creation, she was able to know everything that mattered.

What mattered most to Jessie on this late summer evening was to align herself with Betsy's spirit. Jessie knew how hard it was to be a young girl. Betsy was funny and popular with the other kids. She was a cheerleader, for heaven's sake. But Jessie saw the heartache in her eyes and knew that she was ripe for making bad choices that could ruin the rest of her life. Jessie knew the devil was hard at work in the world, toiling behind the scenes trying to steal everyone's joy and make them miserable. He'd done a bang-up job with Betty and Elmer, who fought half of the time and didn't speak to each other the rest of the time. They were both great people, but Jessie knew they should have *never* married each other, much less tried to raise a passel of girls together. But here they were. Most of the time, they did tolerably well as parents, in Jessie's not-so-humble opinion. But Betsy needed a lift, and Jessie knew this cleaning job offered a tiny window of opportunity to give it to her. She also knew she could blow it if she tried to do it on her own, without a good, long talk with God first.

So Jessie laced up her high-top boots, put on her old red plaid shirt, and shoved on the floppy straw hat she'd inherited from her dad a decade earlier. She grabbed her shillelagh and bounded out the door, the long-legged, floppy-eared hound at her side. She whistled as she took long strides in the direction of the forestry. On the way, she passed many homes with neighbors sitting on front porches. A few dogs barked and snarled at Goober, but Goober just wagged his tail and stayed by her side. He knew that his trips to the forestry were far more important than fighting with those curs.

Mr. Truman, the milkman, was sitting on his front porch, his customary spot this time of the evening. "Howdy, Miz Jenkins. Nice evening," he said as he tipped his hat.

"Sure is, Mr. Truman."

"Winning any cases these days?"

"Only the ones that matter," she said. They had the same exchange every time she walked by. She looked forward to it, and so did he.

Before too long, they made it to the entrance of the forestry. Jessie loved this little patch of woods, with its few wooden picnic tables scattered here and there, and one little shelter decked out with a stone fireplace and chimney and tin roof. There were wide walking paths, but very few people ever came here, especially after dark.

"Okay, Papa, here we are. I've got this burden for that sweet little darlin' Betsy Boopie. She's got that great laugh and a high spirit that makes so many people so happy. But Betty has just gone too far this time. You know that the last three times I was over there, Betsy was in tears, and we heard Betty talking to her something terrible. Why, I wouldn't talk to my worst enemies like that, and You know my enemies are some really bad eggs. Now, I want You to show Betty that what she's doing to that little sweetie is just plain wrong. You've got to burden her with it so bad she just has to stop it. And in the meantime, help that little cutie to develop an immunity to that kind of venom. It would be especially great if You would give my Betsy girl ears that always hear You more clearly than anything negative or unkind. And please help that wretched nephew of mine. He's not hopeless, but he's about as close to it as a man can get. He's arrogant, opinionated, and selfish. He doesn't appreciate his family nearly like he should. Oh, he buys them nice clothes and takes them to fancy restaurants, but he doesn't *see* them or really *hear* them. Please give him eyes to see the treasure he has in all five of those beautiful gals of his. Help him get his durn priorities straight! Oops, sorry about that. I know You hate it when I cuss. I'm working hard on that one."

By the time Jessie had worn herself and Goober out, it was completely dark except for a half moon and a sprinkling of stars. She found her favorite old log to sit on beside the little pond in the middle of the forestry. She sat there for a while listening to the birds and the breeze, drinking in God's peace. After a while, she sighed long and loud. She got up, brushed off her dungarees, and said, "Thanks, Papa. It's so good to visit with You and find out what I'm supposed to be doing in this crazy world. Come on, Goober Boy, let's head home. I could eat a horse."

When they finally got home, around eight thirty, she was delighted that she had remembered to pick up a pound of bologna and cheese from the market and a loaf of bread from D'Angelo's Bakery. That and a couple of bottles of soda, and she was in hog heaven.

6

September had come and gone in a blur for Betty. With all four girls in school, she had more time than she'd had in years. Now that her plan for a career of her own had gone down the drain, she found less and less satisfaction in the daily chores of keeping house. She longed for something to fill her time other than dusting and cooking. There were only so many new dishes to try, and she'd already painted almost every piece of furniture in the house. Although, while sitting at the dining room table and looking at her latest project, an old table Annie had given her, Betty felt a small surge of pride. She had painted that old table red with gold antiquing, a new technique that she just loved. She hoped to use it on several more projects soon.

The sound of loud knocking at the back door jolted her out of her daydream. She quickly got up to see who it was. Through the window in the back door, she could see Floyd Blomer, the client Elmer had just gotten out of murder-for-hire charges. Betty cringed and wished she could avoid talking to the lying, cheating scoundrel. But she knew he'd already seen her through the glass, so she threw back her shoulders and opened the door. The Reverend Blomer was a short, bloated, nearly bald man almost fifty years old, but he dyed his hair dark brown and combed the few long, straggly strands from back to front over the top of his baldness. The combover couldn't hide the fact that he was bald any more than that hung jury could ever convince anyone in this town that he hadn't tried to hire that young man to murder his wife, Francie.

It was all over town, and Betty absolutely hated being the object of so much gossip. As if she had any control over her husband! No matter how much Elmer wanted to win every case, and no matter how much he was willing to grandstand in front of juries to get the verdict he wanted, she knew he would never do anything downright crooked. At least she hoped not.

Anyway, Betty opened the door and asked the reverend how she could help him. In his drawn-out twang and with a smile that made Betty want to slap him, he said, "Well, hello there, Miz Lupeny. Here is the milk Mr. Truman left on your steps. Mighty fine to see you looking so lovely on this gorgeous fall mornin'."

It was all Betty could do not to roll her eyes and slam the door. But she bit her tongue, took the wire basket of glass milk bottles, and calmly said, "Yes, it is a beautiful day. Now. What do you need?"

"Oh, I am in need of nothing, my dear lady. Our heavenly Father has so richly supplied all my needs. But I was hoping it would not be too much of an imposition for me to come in and give you a pamphlet that tells all about the new ladies' group we're starting down at the church."

Betty told him that she regularly attended the First Baptist Church and did not want to attend anywhere else.

"Oh, of course, I would never try to get anyone to abandon their church. No. No sirree. You just keep on going to that Baptist church. I merely want you to know about the amazing good works this fine ladies' group is doing on behalf of the unfortunates in our locality. Why, it is just a pure miracle how much money they've been able to bring in to do the Lord's work. Now, if I can just come inside, I'll tell you all about it."

Betty held the door firm as he tried to squeeze his greasy way past her. "I am so sorry, Reverend. I'm sure your ladies do wonders, but I will not be able to join them. The girls keep me much too busy to join any groups."

"Miz Lupeny, there's always time for the Lord's work. But, if you insist, I will defer to you and leave you with this informational pamphlet that will tell you all about the unfortunates we are helping through our little ladies' group. And since I can't convince you to join, you can give your beautiful daughters the opportunity to join our junior ladies' group. Or you can just donate anytime you like. Then you, too, will be doing the Lord's work even though you don't feel like you have time right now."

Betty's eyes narrowed, and her cheeks flushed. "Reverend, if you think I'm going to let my daughters have any part of your charlatan church, you are more deluded than I realized. I may not go around flaunting my religion, but I know a fake when I see one. Good day!" She slammed the door and turned around before she said any more. The nerve! Just because Elmer had represented that sleazeball didn't mean she had to put up with his money-grubbing innuendos. She had always suspected him of skimming money for his fancy suits and Cadillacs from all of the fund-raisers he advertised all over town, sending kids door-to-door and having his ladies call on their friends with his stories of desperate need in places too far away for anyone here to know whether the money was being used as he said or not.

Before Betty got to the kitchen, the phone rang. She hurried past the small Formica kitchen table into the living room with the big maple dining room table. Just around the corner from the kitchen was the small telephone table. She picked up the phone receiver and said, "Hello."

"Oh, Betty, I'm so glad I caught you at home," said Sara Belle Nolan, the mayor's wife, in her exaggerated Southern drawl. "I just drove by and saw Reverend Blomer leaving your house. He was talking to himself and seemed absolutely put out about something. I called just as soon as I got home to be sure there's nothing wrong that I should know about."

"No, Sara Belle, everything's fine. He was just making his rounds trying to drum up business for the 'unfortunates,'" Betty explained as nicely as she could, while rolling her eyes.

"Well, I slowed down to see if there were any other cars at your house, just in case there was something going on that the mayor and I should know about," she quipped.

"Yes, Sara Belle, if anything happens, you'll be the first to know. Oh my, I have to take that pie out of the oven now. Catch you later." Betty hung up the phone and shook her head. "Oh, Lord, have mercy," she prayed out loud. Although Betty regularly attended the big, socially connected church on South Main Street with Elmer and the girls, she had never been able to understand what all the fuss was about. She never went a day without needing to talk to God several times, but every church service she'd ever attended had left her sleepy and bored.

Sara Belle and Mitchell Nolan lived a few blocks down the street, and Betty swore that Sara Belle made up excuses to drive past Betty's house just to spy on her. Because her husband was the mayor, Sara Belle was on every committee in town, which was simply her way of marshaling gossip about everyone else while making herself seem all important. Betty had no use for gossips or snobs, and Sara Belle was the queen of the gossiping snobs. So far this year, Betty had successfully avoided all of Sara Belle's invitations to her endless parties, but she knew they'd have to make an appearance soon. Elmer was the city attorney, and he played poker with the mayor and several others at the Elks lodge every Thursday afternoon. Betty cringed when she remembered the last party she and Elmer had attended at their house.

Betty and Elmer had accepted the Nolans' invitation to their New Years' Eve party last year. The girls had all gone to stay with Elmer's parents, and Betty thought it would be fun to have a night out wearing her fancy red dress and high heels instead of the slacks and flats she wore around the house. But the party had been too loud, with too many people trying to outdo each other. None of Betty and Elmer's close friends were there.

They tried to talk to Mayor Nolan, but Sara Belle kept interrupting to have him come greet someone else who'd just arrived.

They eventually sat down next to Harrison Carter, an older attorney from Crawford, and his wife, Iris. Harrison and his wife were wealthy and had no children. Betty and Elmer loved to hear about their frequent trips abroad. That night, however, Iris was irritated that the mayor had asked them to donate to the Widows and Orphans Fund.

"The nerve!" Iris whispered loudly to Betty. "This is a social gathering, and I for one do not appreciate being hit up for donations when I am invited to what's supposed to be a pleasant evening out."

Harrison nodded in agreement. "I would never donate a dime to that fund. There hasn't been an accounting for several years." Harrison kept track of all the spending and other important business in the towns of Benjamin County, knowing that his wealthy business clients depended on him to protect their interests.

As the night wore on, Elmer and Betty each circulated through the crowd. Betty had a couple of drinks but still felt out of place among so many people trying to impress each other. A few minutes before midnight, Betty tripped over something on her way to the bathroom, upsetting the dessert table. She ended up on the floor with cake, frosting, pie, and whipped cream from head to toe. Worst of all, she broke the heel of one her new sparkly, silver high heels and ripped the seam out of her dress. She and Elmer tried to laugh and make light of the fiasco, but they both knew that everyone there began ripping them to pieces as soon as they left.

7

Maudie Chaplain looked up from her desk on the small back porch she had converted to an office. The desk, an old rolltop her friend Jessie had given her decades ago, was piled high with papers on either side of her and in every nook and cranny. One of the drawers was pulled halfway out, revealing another messy pile of papers. Maudie watched her big, fat tabby cat stalking some poor unsuspecting bird. It was early October, cold and gray outside. Maudie was trying to piece together the comings and goings of Mayor Nolan. Maudie knew she'd figure it out soon enough. She always did.

At sixty-two years old, Maudie still felt alive and full of energy, but just about everyone around her, especially anyone younger, considered her irrelevant, washed up, and useless. Maudie felt invisible. For a while, after her kids grew up and moved out, she had felt abandoned and useless. But eventually she shook off the poor me attitude. When she came back up for air, she realized that she had a golden opportunity to do what she'd always dreamed about. She became a private detective at the ripe old age of fifty-nine. Of course, most of her family and friends thought she'd finally gone completely off the deep end. But she figured she only had one life to live, and if she was going to be invisible, she might as well make some money along the way.

Her current assignment was a real humdinger. Her friend Jessie was an attorney. A fine, honest attorney who had had to scrape and claw for everything she had, too. Jessie had hired Maudie to find out if Mayor Nolan was stealing money from the Widows and Orphans Fund he had set up and administered for nearly all of his fifteen-year tenure as mayor. Everyone in Beacon knew that Mayor Nolan was a crook, but hardly anyone cared. Heck, if he kept the streets clean and free from potholes, he could do whatever else he liked as far as most people were concerned.

Maudie had never liked Mitchell. They had gone to grade school together in Arkansas, before Maudie's family moved to Beacon when she was in high school. Maudie knew Mitchell was nothing but a scheming, conniving blowhard who only wanted to be a big shot so he could order others around and take all the glory. Somehow, he had managed to convince almost everyone in Beacon that he was God's gift to the little town. Maudie and Jessie knew better, but they had always kept their mouths shut, only talking to each other about their suspicions.

Recently, however, Jessie had inadvertently learned from a client about Mitchell frequenting a high-stakes poker game in a nearby county, betting and often losing huge sums of money. Jessie's client, a water department clerk, had told Jessie about this because she wanted Jessie to sue Mitchell for groping her and forcing himself on her at a Christmas party the year before. The lady hadn't wanted to go to the state's attorney to press charges because she knew he was thick as thieves with the mayor. She wanted Jessie to sue the mayor, but Jessie knew she didn't have enough evidence to win. When the lady mentioned the poker game, Jessie knew she'd hit the jackpot.

Maudie looked back at the pile of papers on her desk and decided to get herself a cup of tea. She had lived alone for over two decades, since her youngest child had moved out in 1941. At that time, Maudie had been working full-time as the postmistress for Beacon, a job she loved. She had her cats and her books to keep her company. She had family and friends like Jessie with whom she loved to spend time. She had never been lonely, and she didn't give a second thought to the hard times she'd been through. Hard times were a part of life, nothing to cry about, just a reason to work harder.

Maudie had no truck with folks simpering over her, telling her how sorry they were when her husband died in that terrible mine accident. Heckfire, she was sorry, too, and she had cried herself to sleep every night for nearly a year after he died. She still loved Hank and knew she would till the day she died. But just because he'd died and left her pregnant with their fourth child didn't mean people should feel sorry for her. Nope, she didn't want their sympathy. A bag of potatoes or a load of coal for her stove would have done just fine. Many people had rallied around her in that terrible winter of 1922. It was so cold and damp in her little house back then, with just a coal stove for heat. She had no idea how she'd survive or keep her kids fed, but she prayed every night and got up every morning determined to make ends meet. And she always did. Not because she worked her fingers to the bone, but because the good Lord had seen fit to be merciful.

Those first years after Hank died were a blur. She was still amazed they had survived. She'd had the little house she still lived in, a rooster, two hens, some canning from the summer before, and an iron and ironing board. Her brother brought her a bag of groceries and a gallon of milk every other week when he got paid. Her church paid her real estate taxes for the first two years, and her sister came to help her with the other kids when the baby was born. That first spring, when the baby was four months old and still nursing, she started selling eggs and taking in ironing to make a little money to buy shoes and coats for the kids. She had an old sewing machine, and sometimes her neighbor, who had a little fabric store, brought her the end pieces from her reams so she could make clothes for the kids. She knew she was a terrible seamstress, but she forged ahead and made them all clothes to keep them covered as best she could.

When Joey, the baby, had gone to school in 1928, she'd had the great fortune of being hired as Beacon's first female postmistress. The former postmaster, old Harold Beams, was getting ready to retire at the end of the year, and his wife, Mable, was one of Maudie's best ironing customers. Mable told Maudie to apply for the job, and Maudie surprised herself and everyone else when she showed up at the post office in a spiffy, new navy-blue skirt and jacket, looking very pulled together and professional. She had convinced Mr. Beams that his beloved post office would be well cared for in her hands.

Maudie came back to her desk with her cup of tea, ready to go over her notes again, but was interrupted by the phone ringing. She got up and walked through her cluttered little home to the hallway, muttering as she went, "That darn phone. Wish I'd never agreed to install it. Hello, Maudie Chaplain here."

"Maudie, gal, you won't believe it, but we've got him by the ying-yangs this time for sure. He left a trail we can follow as sure as if he'd dripped blood all the way from the crime scene. Now, here's the plan..." Jessie fairly tripped over her words she was so excited.

When she could finally get a word in edgewise, Maudie agreed to go with Jessie to the Bocce Lodge, where they'd have a beer to celebrate the mayor's impending demise. The Bocce was a private drinking establishment with members of both high and low class. The lower-class, working folks liked it because the booze was cheap, and the bocce ball court was always open and free. The upper-class members liked it because they considered it private enough to talk about their important business without being overheard. Everyone knew what happened at the Bocce stayed at the Bocce. Otherwise, the other members quickly terminated your membership and ostracized you from all other social gatherings, as well. No one in the small town of Beacon wanted to be given the cold shoulder wherever they went, so everyone had always stayed quiet.

The mayor's best friend, Judge Horton Terrance, went to the Bocce every Wednesday night while his wife went to evening services at the Abundant Life

Church on South Main Street. Mrs. Terrance proudly told her pastor and church friends that Judge Terrance was much too busy to attend church in the middle of the week, poor dear. Everyone but her knew he went straight to the Bocce every Wednesday at 5 p.m. sharp.

The Bocce's longtime bartender, grill cook, janitor, and bocce tournament organizer, Phil Gordon, known and loved by all as Gordie, had been Jessie's client decades ago, when he was in his twenties and too naïve to know that crime most definitely did not pay, at least not in the long run. Gordie had to do a few months in the pen for robbing a local gas station after getting drunk with his buddies. Jessie hadn't gotten him off completely, but she'd listened to him and got him a better deal than he'd expected. When he got out of the pen, Jessie had wheeled and dealed again, this time convincing the Bocce leaders to give Gordie a chance by hiring him. Gordie slept in a little bedroom at the back of the bar, cooked all his meals there, and took his showers at his sister's house next door.

Gordie had been there about a dozen years by 1962. He knew everyone and all their secrets. He never spilled a word to anyone, not even Jessie. But Jessie knew how to ask questions without anyone knowing they were being interrogated. Without realizing it, Gordie had given Jessie enough facts to piece together with other information so that she and Maudie had almost figured out the mayor's scheme.

They knew that Judge Terrance was in cahoots with the mayor in his rotten embezzling scheme. Sure, the judge wasn't taking any money himself, but he knew the mayor had been skimming that fund as if it was his own for years. Judge Terrance loved to drink Irish whiskey and tell stories about his cases, making everyone at the Bocce laugh at his raucous wit. Of course, they laughed a bit harder and louder at his jokes than at regular folks' jokes, but the Honorable Judge Terrance was far too enamored of himself to see that. Sometimes, the Honorable forgot where he was and who was around and said quite a bit more than he remembered the next day. Mayor Nolan never came in on Wednesday nights because he always attended services at the largest and most prestigious church in town, the Immaculate Baptist Church on North Main Street. Mayor Nolan was a deacon there and prided himself greatly on his perfect attendance and spotless record of heading every major committee at some time during his forty years of membership.

Jessie and Maudie arrived at six thirty that evening, after the judge had finished his meal of corned beef and cabbage and begun his real drinking for the night. As usual, the judge was at his table at the back end of the

bar, right next to the barstools and the draft-beer spig-
ots, where Gordie sat on his stool when not serving customers. The gals pulled up barstools close to the judge's
table, greeted the judge and his drinking buddies, and
ordered two beers.

"Good to see you gals. Whatcha want tonight?" asked
Gordie in his soft Midwestern drawl. Gordie had laid
off the booze for a decade now, but having drunk much
more than his share for at least twenty years before
that, he had fully and permanently pickled all but a few
of his precious brain cells. Gordie was kind and amiable
and would give anyone the shirt off his back, which was
all he owned, but no one had ever accused him of being too smart for his own good. Maudie ordered a draft
beer and Jessie ordered a can of Stag.

"Lordy, how do you drink that swill?" asked Maudie
for the hundredth time. Jessie just shook her head and
said, "Got a taste for it when I was poor, and now it
makes me feel rich, sweetie."

Jessie was the only female attorney in Beacon, working in a totally chauvinistic judicial system. Judge Terrance didn't exactly respect her, but he always acted
friendly to her, just as he did to everyone. The Honorable was first and last a politician. Judging cases was
just a sideline. His real gig was powerbroking every
election in their little county. He spent much more

time meeting with elected officials and wannabes than he did presiding over cases. He prided himself for being in on every major and most minor deals in what he considered to be the well-oiled political machine of Benjamin County, where it was political suicide to run as a Republican.

Mayor Nolan would still be filling prescriptions in his dusty little pharmacy if the Honorable hadn't greased the wheels to get him elected in 1948. The Honorable knew that Nolan had faked a limp and other maladies to get out of serving in World War II, a fact otherwise known in Beacon only to his wife, and of course, to Maudie and Jessie. Both Mitchell and Sara Belle Nolan had grown up in Arkansas, and both had wealthy parents who made sure they had the best of everything. Unfortunately, neither family had ever bothered themselves with morals or integrity. They were entitled, and that was all that mattered. Mitchell was not going to get involved with something as dirty and degrading as fighting a war, so he faked illnesses. The draft board officer was all too happy to take a nice vacation that year for the first time in a decade.

Mitchell and Sara Belle hadn't planned on having to work to earn a living, but Mitchell's parents stuck to the only parenting rule that could have made a man out of their son. He would get an education and become a professional, only able to inherit from them if he carried on the Nolan tradition of becoming a pillar in his community. Mitchell felt terribly mistreated when he realized they weren't kidding. After just barely graduating from college with a degree in pharmacy, he and Sara Belle came to Beacon, where Mitchell took over the pharmacy Sara Belle's uncle had opened years earlier.

Mitchell hated everything about being a pharmacist, but most of all, he hated hearing about every little ache and pain of every little old lady in town. Heavens, he couldn't walk to the square without someone stopping him to tell him in excruciating detail about their hemorrhoids or troubled bowels. They all disgusted him, and he couldn't care less about any of it, but he acted interested and gave them whatever answer he thought they wanted to hear, and then made an excuse to get away from them as quickly as possible. He became very adept at fooling almost everyone into thinking that he actually cared about them, a quality he found to be quite useful when he got into politics.

At the Bocce, after Jessie and Maudie sipped their beers for a while, they heard the judge tell his audience, "You'll have to excuse me, fellows. I hear my easy chair and pipe calling me."

Before the judge got up from his chair, Jessie had ordered another round for the table. She turned around on her stool and raised her beer to the judge. "I was hoping to toast your anniversary, Judge. Can you stay for another round?"

The judge looked at Jessie as if he didn't know what she meant. Then he quickly and loudly told Gordie to match Jessie's offer by sending everyone in the house another round on him. "Everyone" consisted of two old guys playing checkers and a young man at the bar wearing his gas station coveralls. Jessie called out in her best, booming courtroom voice, "Now, that's more like it, Judge." She and Maudie handed the glasses to the table. When Jessie was sure everyone was listening, she stood up and raised her beer. "To the finest judge in Southern Illinois. May the past fifteen years spent serving Benjamin County as our resident circuit court judge be a feather in your cap and a springboard for many happy years to come." She clinked her beer to the judge's glass and drank a long swig in his honor before turning around and winking at Maudie.

Through it all, Maudie quietly observed everything. She noticed that the old guys playing checkers were mostly silent, but occasionally talked quietly across the table. Earnest Pavlis, a poor farmer whose wife had been seriously ill, kept running his gnarly, shaking hand through the back of his thin, scraggly hair. His buddy, Calvin Dooley, a cab driver, kept stealing looks at Earnest when he was studying the board, as if he was concentrating on their game. Calvin's eyes bored into Earnest, but Calvin always smiled and made a little joke when Earnest looked up at him. They'd been buddies all their lives.

The young man at the bar, Marty O'Keefe, came from a "bad" family. His older brother was in and out of jail all the time. Soon, the brother would find his way to the state penitentiary, where his uncle had been for the past six years. Maudie had known Marty's mom, Clara, since Marty, the youngest of three boys, was seven. Clara was widowed when her boys were young, and she and Maudie had been friends through the years of raising their kids on their own. Maudie knew that Marty, now twenty-two years old, was determined to break out of the O'Keefe mold and live a decent life, but he'd just been rebuffed by a girl he was dying to go out with. Maudie prayed silent prayers for all of them, just as she had done all her life. Praying for the needs of others was the real work of her life. Being a postmistress and now old lady detective were just her vocations.

Jessie plied the Honorable with drinks, asking him questions about himself as if nothing else in life interested her more. It was far too easy to convince him of this. Jessie had long ago learned how to get information out of people by playing to their egos, and the Honorable's ego was so huge it had swallowed him whole about five minutes after he ascended to the bench.

After a half hour of smiles and "Well, how about that, Judge," and "I never knew that! What happened next?" Jessie was worn out but delighted at her haul of information. She and Maudie made excuses about having to get home for this or that. On the way out, Jessie shook Gordie's hand and quietly asked him to call her tomorrow. She knew she'd be able to piece together the rest of the puzzle after talking to him.

As Jessie drove Maudie back to her little house, they intently recounted the information the judge had unknowingly divulged. Now they knew that the mayor's poker games were always held on the third Thursday of the month in the back room of a seedy tavern on the outskirts of Crawford, right after the banks delivered that month's money for the Widows and Orphans Fund.

Soon after the mayor proclaimed the Fund, he had convinced all three of the local banks to offer a special savings account, similar to a Christmas Club, for their patrons. It had been wildly popular in Beacon, and soon the practice spread to some of the other banks in the county, and most of the churches collected an offering once a year for the Fund. The mayor had made several speeches pleading on behalf of the poor widows and orphans who needed his assistance, encouraging everyone, including little children, to donate something every month. "Every penny counts!" was his motto. The *Beacon Inquirer*, the only daily newspaper in the county, had made a deal with the mayor to collect donations for the Fund when they collected for the newspaper subscriptions. Lots of cash flowed in every month, and the mayor had convinced the rubber-stamping city council that he should relieve them of the time-consuming job of administering the Fund. Consequently, he was the sole bean counter.

Every year, the mayor wrote a long article in the paper about all the widows and orphans his Fund had helped, how their lives might have been lost but for his assistance. The paper always published at least one large photo of a pitifully grateful widow standing next to the beaming mayor as he gave the poor woman a large cardboard check with the amount given clearly visible.

For the past five years or more, however, both Jessie and Maudie had heard lots of complaints from widows they knew about how complicated the application forms had become. All of them knew they had filled out the forms correctly, but all had been denied assistance due to some technical mistake. All were encouraged to apply again. Neither Jessie nor Maudie knew anyone who had actually been assisted in that time. They figured the mayor chose one or two families to give some of the Fund money to, made a big deal out of it, and that lulled the public into feeling good about how much they had helped the mayor help the needy. Once lulled, most of the public didn't really care what actually happened to the money.

But Jessie and Maudie weren't like most folks. They had begun digging into things a few months earlier. Maudie had learned from a friend at the newspaper that the Beacon paper boys collected at least two hundred dollars a month for the Fund, and that the adults who delivered the paper by car contributed about half that amount from their rural routes. Maudie's friend wasn't worried that the mayor was skimming the Fund, only that the adult carriers might be stealing from it. Jessie had learned from a treasurer at one of the banks that their W&O Fund collection totaled over three hundred dollars every month. They had both sat in on enough city council meetings to know that the mayor could have pocketed every cent of the Fund's money without a single council member knowing or caring anything about it.

At the Bocce, Jessie and Maudie had also learned that the mayor had just bought a house in Arkansas, a "little ol' hunting lodge," according to the judge. Although the judge had not been there yet, he was sure it was just a little shack for the mayor and his hunting buddies to use, probably not worth the ground it sat on. Jessie and Maudie made plans to find out the truth.

Maudie wasn't trained as a lawyer like Jessie, but she had learned very well how to read people. In her years as a postmistress, she came to know almost all the families in Beacon. She knew where they lived, to whom they were related, where they worked and banked, whether they were in debt or had savings, and whether they were kind- or coldhearted. She would never have opened anyone's mail, but seeing who got what kinds of mail from what kinds of businesses gave her a real good idea of what was going on, especially when the people who were receiving that mail talked to her. She didn't know details or bank balances, but she knew who was down and who was up, who was straight and who was crooked.

After she retired from the post office, she put her knowledge of the people of Beacon to work for her as a detective. At first, Jessie had simply asked her to help get information in one divorce case. Jessie had asked Maudie to find out if the soon-to-be ex-husband was fooling around on Jessie's client. Maudie had slipped around to the places she knew the man would go if his wife's suspicions were correct. Within two weeks, Maudie was able to report back to Jessie that the husband was clearly *not* fooling around. Jessie was sure Maudie hadn't fully understood. She loved Maudie and respected her immensely but was sure Maudie hadn't appreciated the difficulty of the assignment.

Jessie stammered around, trying not to show her disappointment. Finally, Maudie shrugged and explained, "It's incredibly easy to get information from almost anyone when you're just an old lady. All I had to do was go into the bars and motels where Don would have gone and tell them some story about forgetting where I was supposed to meet my nephew, who was coming to town for the first time from Chicago."

Jessie said, "You don't have any nephews, Maudie!"

"But who else knows that?" asked Maudie. "Most of the younger folk don't know me, so it was easy to fib just a little and find out all kinds of stuff. If I knew the folks, I just made up some story that went along with how they knew me and got my information that way. Who would ever suspect that a gray-haired, dumpy, old lady would be a detective?" Maudie smiled slyly. She knew she ought to feel bad about telling so many lies, but she was exhilarated and not the least bit remorseful.

Jessie looked at her quizzically for a few seconds. Jessie was almost never at a loss for words, but she was stumped. Who would have ever thought that her sweet, quiet, pious friend would turn out to be a top-notch detective? "Well, if that don't beat all!" Jessie laughed and shook her head. Then Maudie started laughing. Then they really started laughing, hooting, and hollering, until they were both crying big crocodile tears. Finally, Maudie managed to say through her laughter, "Yeah, that's me, the invisible sleuth!" And they laughed even louder.

———

As they drove home from the Bocce, she and Jessie planned their next move. Jessie would have Jack check out the poker game and take photos of those coming and going. He would also make a trip down to Arkansas to check out the mayor's little hunting lodge. Maudie would begin going through records at the library of deaths for the past fifteen years. Then she would find out if any of those widows or orphans had applied for assistance from the fund and whether any of them had received any money. Maudie knew she had her work cut out for her because many of them would have moved or be hard to find for a million different reasons. She would go to the churches and other places they had frequented. Maudie was excited at the prospect of getting to the bottom of it.

The next morning, Maudie went to the garage where Marty worked, under the not-entirely-untrue ruse that she thought her brakes were going out. Maudie had learned to fix just about everything in her house over the years, but she had not had time to learn auto mechanics. She had not even learned to drive until she retired from the post office.

Marty came out to her car, wiping his greasy hands on an old rag. His wavy brown hair stuck out all around the old ball cap sitting backward over his rugged face. Maudie studied him as he walked toward her. She saw his determination mixed with a heavy dose of defeat. "Good mornin', ma'am. Whatcha need?"

"Well, I know you're busy, but I wonder if you could check out the brakes on this old jalopy. They seem awfully loose recently."

Marty didn't hesitate. He asked if he could drive her car himself, and Maudie gladly agreed. She went around to the passenger side and got in beside him. They drove out of the lot onto East Main Street, heading toward the Square. As they drove, Maudie asked him about his life. Before they got back to the shop, Maudie had not only learned what she had come to find out, but she also found out that Marty wanted to date a younger girl Maudie knew through Jessie.

Marty assured Maudie that her brakes were fine for the time being but told her to come back right away if they got any worse. Before she drove off, she asked Marty to come to dinner Sunday after church, knowing that he wouldn't accept any money for his help with her car. He gratefully accepted the invitation to lunch. Maudie laughed out loud as she drove off. Little did Marty know, the girl he was pining over would be there, too. Jessie had recently hired the girl part-time, and they were coming over for lunch before her first day. Of course, Jessie was just taking the girl under her wing. Her parents were longtime clients of Jessie's and were concerned that their high school daughter had too much time on her hands.

8

It was a lovely, bright, crisp October evening when Elmer, Betty, and the girls loaded into the sedan to head to Raymond's Tavern for Friday night fish. They had to get there in plenty of time for Elmer to get back to Beacon to announce the home football game. Raymond's was in Simpson, another little town in Benjamin County. There were lots of little towns—Westfort, Simpson, and Crawford were the closest to Beacon. But even though these little towns were all in the same county and state, they were fierce rivals at everything that mattered. Betty had been born and raised in Westfort, and her folks still lived there. She and the girls went to Westfort every week to visit, and they loved the city park. Beacon didn't have any parks, just a couple of dirt fields marked off with painted lines for baseball. Betty's family usually had their good weather gatherings at the Westfort park. This was close to treason for many Beacon old-timers.

Westfort was about seven miles south of Beacon, and Crawford was five miles west. Crawford was much smaller than Westfort or Beacon; only about a thousand people lived there. But Crawford was a real hub for kids all over the county, because they had a bandstand, a lake with a beach, and two drive-in hamburger joints. Beacon had the only drive-in movie theater in the county, though, so kids from all over the county spent at least one night most summer weekends with a carload of kids at the Beacon drive-in, which was also *the* spot for dates, at least for those girls who had permission to go on car dates.

Simpson didn't have much to offer, at least as far as the girls were concerned. Elmer thought differently, as many of his clients lived in Simpson, including Raymond, the owner and "chef" of their favorite Friday night outing. Simpson was just over six miles northeast of Beacon. Raymond's was right on Main Street. But there was hardly any business that wasn't on Main Street in Simpson. As they drove, Betsy and Karen began whispering to each other about something, and Ellie was determined to listen. She had learned long ago that being the youngest had decided advantages. All she had to do was act like she was playing some game or daydreaming or "reading," and all the adults around her would talk about everything as if she wasn't there at all. The minute she asked a question or acted interested, however, they all got quiet or started talking about something else. Ridiculous! Ellie had learned to act like she wasn't paying a bit of attention, and she often heard a lot more than she had bargained for. This evening was no different. As her mom and dad listened to the radio in the front, she sat quietly between her two sisters, "playing" with her troll dolls. Laura was staying overnight at her friend Stella's, so she wasn't there, but she was much too smart to say anything worthwhile in front of Ellie anyway.

Karen whispered breathlessly, "I can't wait to see him tonight. I think we can slip out of the game and make it back before the end. Dad will never know." Ellie knew that Karen was in love with a boy from Crawford, and she also knew that their dad had strictly forbidden Karen from having anything to do with him, saying something about petting, whatever that meant, and driving too fast.

Betsy whispered back, "You can't do that! What if you get caught? You'll be grounded for the rest of the year!" Karen sighed and said, "No way. Tony and I are gonna meet at the concession stand just before halftime and then come back before the end of the game. What could happen?"

Just then, they pulled into the gravel parking lot of Raymond's, a nondescript, two-story brown wooden building. They parked next to Jessie's car, a bright robin's-egg-blue Cadillac Deville convertible. She and Grandma and Grandpa Lupeny pulled in. Everyone got out and hugged and said hello. Grandpa was wearing his "good" overalls and his favorite green plaid shirt. Grandma wore her second-best going-out dress, which was not quite as nice or new as her Sunday dress, but lots nicer and newer than her two everyday dresses. Jessie wore brown slacks, a brown tweed jacket, a bright orange blouse with orange lace ruffles down the front, and a brown-and-green-checked fedora with a bright green feather cocked jauntily over her black hair. Karen and Betsy rolled their eyes and looked at each other in horror. They were constantly mortified at Jessie's outlandish outfits and hats. Ellie ran up to Jessie, and Jessie scooped her up in her lumberjack arms and hugged and kissed her loudly as Ellie squealed with delight.

They went into the side door to avoid the tavern part of the diner. Jessie and Elmer went into the tavern to get beers, and Betty and the others traipsed across the bare wooden floors into the dining room, glad the large table in the middle of the dining room was open. The smell of fish frying, cold beer sloshing, and cigarette smoke was familiar and comforting. The tall, busty, redheaded waitress named Joan gave them their menus, even though hardly anyone ever ordered anything other than fish sandwiches on Friday nights. They ordered sweet tea and sodas and settled in to chat about the happenings of the week as they waited for Elmer and Jessie to return, which they would, soon enough. Otherwise, Grandpa would head into the bar to order a beer, and then Grandma would have to follow him and drag him out by his ear, even though she was almost a foot shorter than him.

Directly, Elmer and Jessie came out of the barroom and took their places. Joan took their orders and left. "Well, I can tell ya'll, I am absolutely tickled pink to see you. I have some *big* news," said Jessie, loudly and with a sly grin. "Betcha can't guess," she taunted with a huge smile. Betsy said, "I know, you've got a boyfriend!"

Jessie laughed and pounded the table. "Whooee! I sure wish that was it, but it's not, unless I've got a secret admirer just waitin' to make me his bride."

Ellie chimed in, "I know! I know! You're going somewhere on the train!" Ellie had overheard Betty talking on the phone about Jessie, saying she ought to get her caboose in line. Jessie shook her head and said, "No, that's a good guess little darlin', but that's not it, either."

Elmer said, "You got a job and are moving to Chicago?" a bit too hopefully.

"Nope, you couldn't make it here without me, nephew," she replied with a wink. "Okay, ya'll give up yet?"

"Yes! Tell us, tell us, Auntie Jessie," yelled Ellie. Betty quietly told her to pipe down.

Just then, their food arrived, and everyone got busy getting ready to eat. Jessie made them stop to say grace, which they never did unless she was with them. They all bowed their heads as Grandma blessed their lives and the food. Jessie looked at them all after the prayer, took a deep breath, and finally said, "I've been invited to go to Rome this December, and I want Annie to go with me."

"Oh, my word!" cried Annie. "How on earth would I ever pay for a trip like that?"

"Well, that's what makes it so great. I have a client with business interests there. He wants to fly me over there to help him with a couple of things, and I need an assistant. I can't take Cookie because I need her to stay here and take care of the rest of my business. So, Annie can go with me instead. Think you can make it on your own for a couple of weeks, Fred?" Jessie asked, knowing that her brother would never say no to her in front of the grandkids.

"Oh, I suppose. She's gonna go no matter what I say anyway. You two gals are always cookin' something up—and I don't mean on no stove, neither," said Fred, acting like he was very put upon, but secretly he was delighted that he'd have the house to himself for a while. Ever since he'd retired from the coal mines a few years earlier, Annie was constantly on him to do a million chores around the house. Fred was already planning to buy a case of beer and several cigars to keep him company in her absence.

Jessie and Annie couldn't contain their giddiness at the prospect of another trip together. Annie absolutely loved to travel and see new places, but Fred complained when they had to go to Simpson for Friday night dinner. Early in their marriage, they had come to a wonderful compromise. Jessie took Annie with her on jaunts and ganders and all sorts of crazy adventures every chance she could. So, this surprise really didn't surprise anyone too much. But it was always fun when they came back, full of stories and presents for all of them.

When they finished their meals, Elmer paid the bill, over Jessie's protests. He was so happy at the prospect of Jessie being away from the office for a couple of weeks that he would have paid for a hundred of her dinners. They said their good-byes outside, but Ellie put her little suitcase into Jessie's car. She was going to stay overnight with Grandma and Grandpa so Elmer and the other girls could go to the football game and Betty could go to "Club." Club was simply a group of Betty's girlfriends who got together once a month to play cards at one of their homes. Ellie sometimes went with Betty, but tonight they were meeting at Helen Hobbie's house. Helen was Stella's mom, and she didn't have any small children for Ellie to play with. But the real reason Ellie wasn't going with Betty tonight was because Helen had just been diagnosed with breast cancer, and her girlfriends wanted to rally around her without being distracted by their kids.

After Aunt Jessie dropped them off, waving "Toodaloo!" out of her car window, Ellie ran into the little green wood frame house through the front screen porch. She hoped she and Grandpa could sleep out there if it wasn't too cold tonight. Grandma put her little suitcase into the spare bedroom and went to the kitchen to fix them all a cup of hot tea with lots of honey. As Grandma fixed their tea, Grandpa turned on the TV to see his favorite show, *Have Gun-Will Travel*. Ellie busied herself with her troll dolls, Maggie and Dirk, a married couple with two little baby trolls, Cindy and Ray-Ray. Ellie loved her grandparents, but she always preferred to be anywhere her big sisters were. That was where the real action was. Ellie knew that high school was the absolute best place ever in the world, and she couldn't wait to get there. Until then, she hung on every word and gesture of her sisters and their friends.

Soon, Grandma came into the living room from the kitchen. Grandma and Grandpa's house was small and messy but clean. Grandma didn't like dirt or dust, but she had so many projects going that she just left them all out so she could work on them when the mood struck. Ellie sat on the floor in front of the divan, which was brown with huge bright green and blue flowers. Grandpa sat in his big easy chair with the matching ottoman, all with green and brown stripes. Grandma had taught herself how to reupholster furniture. All of their furniture was either ancient or cast off from somewhere else but made new by Grandma's magic. She scoured the fabric store for bargains on materials heavy enough to cover furniture, then made coordinating pillows out of old dresses or coats.

Grandma brought Grandpa and Ellie their tea and shortbread cookies, sat down with hers on the divan, and asked Ellie how Maggie and Dirk were doing. "Oh, they're okay now, but it's been a dagnabbit rotten week," Ellie said nonchalantly. Grandma said, "*Tsk, tsk,* child, where did you hear language like that?"

"Auntie Jessie I suppose. I like to listen to her when she gets all riled up about her cases," explained Ellie.

"Well, I'll have to remind her to watch her mouth when she's around you. We don't say 'dagnabbit' here. It's not a nice word," Grandma told her.

Ellie looked puzzled and asked what was wrong with it. Grandpa chimed in and said emphatically, "Not a gosh-darned thing, sweet pea. Now, tell us about those dolls."

Grandma exclaimed, "Fred, not you, too!"

Ellie stood up with Maggie and said in a high, squeaky voice with a pronounced Southern drawl, "I declare, Annie, last week just about did me in, what with all that nonsense about that nice young man runnin' for president. Why, you'd think he'd a shot someone the way they talk about him. And me with company to cook for and Dirk off on his mountain-climbing adventure."

Grandpa laughed and slapped his leg. "Goldarn it, girlie, if you aren't just a rascal! Get over here and give your old grampa a big hug."

Ellie went over to him, and he hugged her tight. "You're my little sunshine, dollie."

"I know, Grandpa. Now, will you help me get Cindy and Ray-Ray dressed up? They've got to get ready for the big school play tomorrow," Ellie said as she went back to her trolls. Grandpa smiled from ear to ear and got down on the floor with her, not giving a second thought to how he was going to get back up again.

Grandma smiled to herself and went to the large, dark wood dining room table that sat between the divan and the arched doorway to the kitchen. On it was a pile of cloth that would be a jacket she was sewing for herself from a picture in the Sears-Roebuck catalog, a tall stack of envelopes that held her precious letters to and from her Japanese pen pal, her very large Bible and notebooks and Catholic Church magazines, and her rusty toolbox with her upholstery tools. Beside the table were her sewing machine, an old bench that she hoped to add a red leatherette seat to next week, and a stack of rags she would reuse for rugs and other projects. Grandma stayed up late every night working on her projects, even upholstering if need be. Once Grandpa fell asleep, he couldn't hear thunder a foot away.

———

At the football stadium, Elmer announced a touchdown by the opposing team, the Westfort Bluejays, Beacon's fiercest rivals. Every game had an intense do-or-die atmosphere, and this one was no different. It was just two minutes before halftime, and all the fans on both sides were on their feet yelling and screaming as the Bluejay player made ready to kick the field goal. If he made it, the game would be tied seven to seven. Karen had made sure her dad saw her with her girlfriends earlier in the game. The announcer's box was at the top center of the home bleachers, and those inside could see only part of the home crowd. Those who sat near the top and farthest to the sides were obscured by the walls of the box. The high school kids all sat on the far-right side, so Karen sat there, too, not wanting to draw any unwanted attention from her dad. Still, Karen knew she had to be very careful.

She was so excited she could hardly breathe. She hoped Tony hurried up from his job at his dad's gas station. He was supposed to get off early tonight so they could be together again. But as Karen waited near the concession stand, Betsy caught her attention and made a motion with her right hand, index finger held out and drawn slowly across her neck, looking as mean and menacing as she could. Karen stuck out her tongue at Betsy and turned around. Karen was wearing that new maroon sweater set Tony said he liked, and she pretended to look at the game schedule, but as she looked up, scanning the gates leading to the street just outside the stadium, anyone with half a brain could tell she was looking for a boy. Karen looked up at the field as she heard her dad's voice across the airwaves, "That's first and ten for the Beacon Rangers! Quarterback Roger Stanton's pass completed to Tommy Janes for a gain of twenty yards!" The home crowd went wild, cheering and clapping and ringing cowbells.

Karen nearly screeched, and she jumped a foot when someone pulled her hair from behind. She swung around and cried, "Oh, Tony, you're here!" wanting so badly to hug and kiss him she could have wept. But, of course, she tried very hard to act as nonchalant as her furiously beating heart would let her. Tony scanned the crowd and said, "Hey, looks like a good game. Wanna stay and watch for a while?" Karen looked up nervously toward the bleachers. "You know we can't do that, Tony," Karen whispered.

"Oh yeah, your old man don't like me. Well, let's book. I been dying to get my hands on you all day," he said. Tony had black hair, slicked back, and he was wearing tight blue jeans, a white T-shirt, a black vinyl leather-look jacket, and shiny black boots. Karen thought he was just the most gorgeous hunk she'd ever seen. Elmer knew he was a thief and that his dad was a drunk, more than enough to make him contemplate murder every time he thought about that punk even looking at his sweet Karen.

Tony grabbed Karen's hand, and they ran out of the gate just as the horn blared announcing the end of the first half. Betsy shook her head as she watched them. She knew she'd have to play lookout for her sister in case their dad came down to the concession stand. She told her group of friends that she had to go find her sister, and they went on laughing and talking, not aware of the drama. Betsy and Karen fought like two cats in a burlap bag when they were at home, but they always looked out for each other. Betsy was smart enough to keep her mouth shut about Karen and Tony. Everyone but Karen knew Tony was a "hood," one of the fast boys that nice girls didn't dare date, at least openly.

Betsy stationed herself at the edge of the concession stand where lots of people milled around and stood in line. That way, her dad couldn't see her from the announcer's booth and would think she was just there with her friends if he came down for a soda.

Up in the announcer's booth, Elmer was in his glory. The Rangers were playing well, and a couple of his poker and drinking buddies had come up to the booth to chew the fat during halftime. Elmer got a break from announcing for most of halftime, right after he told the crowd: "Folks, be sure to get some hot popcorn and cold sodas from the concession stand, but first, enjoy the high school band's incredible halftime show." As he put down his headphones and shut off his mic, he told his buddies Joe and Danny that he'd rather have his ears punctured with an icepick than listen to that crappy band.

Tony drove his souped-up 1959 Chevy Belair that his dad had bought him brand-new for his sixteenth birthday. Karen thought it was dreamy, as did all the other girls Tony dated. Elmer had told her flat-out she was banned from ever getting into that car, whether Tony was in it or not. Of course, that just sealed the deal for Karen, who now wanted nothing more than to be with Tony in his cherry-red hotrod every chance she got.

Tony drove slowly till they got out of town, and then he put the pedal down, squealed the tires, and shot off to the back roads like a whirlwind. Karen didn't like going so fast, but she just clutched the armrest on her door and tried to act like she was having fun. She looked over at Tony and was amazed to see him smiling a decidedly wicked smile.

"Where are we going, Tony? You know I have to be back in forty minutes, don't you?" she asked as lightly as possible.

"Just you wait till I get you out to my dad's farm. You'll never want to come back," Tony said, winking at her.

"Oh, I have always wanted to go out to the farm. I've never seen your dad's horses. I bet they're beautiful. But I have to get back, Tony. If my dad finds out I've been with you, he'll kill me."

"Have it your way, babe. But you don't know what you're missing." Tony turned onto the next side road and pulled around so fast it threw Karen into the middle of the car, almost onto Tony's lap.

"Now, that's more like it. You were practically in Siberia all the way over by the door," Tony said as he put the car into PARK and reached over, trying to kiss her.

"Oh, Tony, you're so funny." Karen laughed nervously, trying to withstand his advance. She was thrilled that he wanted to be with her, but she couldn't get rid of the knot in her stomach. Her mom had always told her to trust her gut, but Karen had been so busy trying to please Tony that she had no idea what her gut was telling her. She finally relented and let him kiss her, but when he tried to undo her bra, she squirmed to get away. "Tony, please stop," she said, almost in tears. Luckily, a car was coming down the road with its bright lights on. That sidetracked Tony, who figured he'd do better anyway if he took this one back to the game early. That way, he could look up that hot new waitress at the Kewpie Café. Suddenly, he was ravenously hungry. "Have it your way, doll," he said nonchalantly as he threw the car into gear and backed out.

Tony raced back to the football field and pulled up at the entryway just as the buzzer rang out announcing that the third quarter was over. Tony leaned over and kissed her until she nearly fainted, then looked her in the eyes and said, "There's more where that came from, darlin'. Just don't keep me waiting too long."

Karen opened the car door and nearly fell down as she got out, her knees were so weak.

Karen didn't realize that Jack Ward lived directly across the street from the football field. He always sat by the window in his little second-story bedroom to watch the football games. He could see just about everything with his binoculars. He had just come back from getting a cold beer when he heard the loud muffler of Tony's car pull up. Jack knew Tony and his dad. He had nothing against Tony's old man, Bud Durham, but he had no misconceptions that he was anything but a well-off shyster who had spoiled his son rotten. Jack had been watching Tony for months, ever since Jessie had mentioned that he'd been sniffing around Karen.

After Tony sped away from the football field, Jack went downstairs, got in his old rambler, and headed for the liquor store at the north edge of town. If he was lucky, he'd catch Tony buying booze illegally. Tony was only nineteen years old, but he had been buying booze there for the past two years. The owner was tight with Bud and did whatever Bud told him to do. Most of the local cops were just as bad and wouldn't pick up Tony if they saw him commit murder. But Bud had gotten on the wrong side of Sheriff Lane, so Jack knew he could put a kink in Tony's tail if he watched him long enough.

After Karen got back to the football field, Betsy grabbed her arm just as she floated by. "Oh boy, you've got it really bad, Karen," said Betsy, dragging her toward the bleachers. Betsy knew she had to get her sister up to the stands right away, make sure their dad saw her, and then sit her down to chew her out—again. That creep Tony would get them all grounded if Karen didn't snap out of it, and fast! They walked past the middle of the bleachers, and Betsy waved at her dad until he gave her a nod. Then they went to the kids' section of the bleachers and sat down.

Betsy reminded Karen about all the awful things they'd heard about Tony. She whispered furiously under her breath, hoping no one around heard what she was saying. "Don't you remember that girl from Crawford who's younger than you? He got her pregnant, then dropped her like a hot potato! And everyone knows he stole that motorcycle from Jimmy Neal!" Tony believed that Jimmy had gone out with a girl Tony thought he should have first dibs on. "Everyone but you knows he's nothing but trash," Betsy warned. Karen just stared off into space with a breathy smile. She didn't hear a word her sister said.

9

Laura and Stella sat on the floor of Stella's upstairs bedroom, beside the bed, looking out the window at the trees in the late evening sun. Stella had a pile of used tissues beside her and clutched a pink, heart-shaped pillow. Laura loved her friend Stella and usually felt more peaceful in her little bedroom than anywhere else. Not knowing what to say, Laura looked around the room at the old pink roses on the wallpaper, each one faded but lovely. Stella's princess dresser and bed fit perfectly, giving the girls just enough room to lean up against the bed and put their feet on the window seat looking out onto Stella's backyard. On the dresser, in front of a large mirror, a tray held neatly arranged old perfume bottles her mom had collected for her, none with any perfume but all holding the memories of the women who had used them. Stella's fancy brush and hand mirror sat beside her little jewelry box and the spray bottle of Adorn hairspray that every high school girl they knew used generously before going anywhere in public.

Stella was a lovely, lithe, dark-haired, long-legged girl who loved her mother more than anyone else in the world, and now her world seemed to have crashed down around her. Laura was beautiful in her own way, not nearly as stunning as Stella, but neither of them had an inkling of the power of their beauty. They both thought of themselves as merely ordinary girls. They were best friends, and they shared all their secrets with each other. Laura knew from thousands of hours of heart-to-heart talks that Stella just needed Laura to be with her as she processed the shock of learning that her mom had cancer.

"Oh, Laura, I am so scared I can't stand it. If I lose her, I'll die, too. I know I will," Stella cried, putting her head on her pillow and weeping with ragged breaths. Laura put her hand on Stella's arm and sat there for several minutes, waiting for Stella to get through this round of tears. When the weeping softened and Stella's breaths became more even and calm, Laura said, "We will get through this—together. I don't know how now, but your mom needs you now more than ever, and you won't let her down. Your brothers and your dad need you, too. So, we will be strong together. I promise." Laura had made up her mind before coming to Stella's that evening. She was going to be the rock that Stella could lean on no matter what happened. It wasn't until she went home the next day that Laura silently cried herself to sleep, so overwhelmed with sadness for her friend and the cruel futility of life.

———

Downstairs, the club ladies had all arrived. Betty had arrived early to help Helen get ready. Club nights were sacred to this group of girlfriends. There were always at least eight of them, sometimes as many as fourteen. They had all known each other most of their adult lives and had been getting together at each other's houses every month for over a decade. They all had husbands and school-age kids. Only a few of them worked, and two of them worked for their husbands' businesses. Their dependence on their husbands and position in society as housewives was a frequent topic of conversation, which was why these nights were strictly for them. No men allowed! They all loved their kids, and most of them loved their husbands, but they all wished they had something to call their own. Like most of them, Betty had tried church work, gardening, decorating, cooking, and all manner of projects shown in the women's magazines. But she still felt like she was missing something. Helen was the only one who had a career—she was a registered nurse at the Benjamin Hospital—and now here she was, the one who would have to walk away from the job she loved to face what Betty feared was a death sentence.

The women all sat in Helen's big living room, with little plates of food mostly untouched. They all wore nice clothes, mostly pastel wool slacks and sweater sets. A couple of them had on plaid skirts. They had all taken off their shoes, and they sat around the room on all of the chairs and the floor around the coffee table. Several of them smoked cigarettes, and all had drinks nearby. They didn't come to Club to get drunk. Tonight, though, Betty had known they would all feel shaky and off-center, so she had raided Elmer's liquor cabinet, bringing the bottles and mixers with her. She had poured each of them a drink of their choice. Betty stood in the corner between the dining room and living room, watching to see if anyone needed anything. She had designated herself as the substitute hostess, and she was grateful to have something to focus on other than the awful news Helen was sharing.

Helen sat in the middle of the sofa, with Louise Patton on one side and Florence Bartoni on the other. Helen had just celebrated her forty-third birthday, but tonight she looked more like sixty-three. She had always been slender with light brown hair and translucent skin. Now she seemed to have shrunk several inches, and her eyes were hollow with dark circles underneath. She had found out that she had cancer earlier that week after going to see her doctor about losing weight and feeling tired all the time. Louise was a large, tall woman. She was significantly overweight, but she always dressed and styled her hair impeccably and carried herself with such grace and dignity that no one who knew her well ever thought of her as fat.

Louise had listened with all the others to Helen's brave words about the upcoming surgery and treatment options she faced. Helen paused, and the rest of them were silent for a long while, until Louise hugged Helen tightly and said, "Oh honey, this is just another bump in the road. We'll all be there with you every step of the way."

Florence was a petite, round lady with a quick wit and a cheerful smile, but tonight she had started crying as soon as Helen told them the news. She was still cryingas Louisehugged Helen. "Well, all I know is that I am going to start praying right now, and I'm not going to stop praying until you are healed and this nightmare ends," Florence exclaimed in her soft, girlish voice. All the others agreed and began talking at once, saying how they would pray and help out in any way they could.

Helen thanked them, and then Betty said, "Okay, we've done all we can about this tonight. Let's get our minds on something else. How about some pinochle, girls?"

"Hallelujah, I thought you'd never ask," said Helen, and they all laughed much too hard as they began moving toward the large dining room table for the game.

A week later, Betty was finishing the birthday dinner she had prepared for Laura's seventeenth birthday. The family was all coming over to help celebrate. This was just the second time after Laura's surgery that they'd been able to have a real birthday party for her. Laura had scoliosis and had to have major back surgery the summer before her freshman year of high school. Then she had been in a cast that covered her from her neck to her thighs. They had installed a hospital bed in Laura's bedroom, where she had stayed that whole school year. Laura had not complained once, but Betty knew it was a terrible ordeal for a young girl to go through. Whether she complained or not, Laura still had to endure a sort of imprisonment that Betty feared would leave a worse scar than the surgery had.

Laura's friends had been her saving grace. Two or more of them stopped by every day after school to bring her books and assignments. And one student in each of her classes was assigned to take the two-way radio from room to room for each of Laura's classes. Laura could hear her teacher and anything the other students said, and she could even ask questions herself. Laura could hardly wait for those afternoon visits. Stella and Meryl Sue and whoever else stopped by kept her up-to-date on all the best gossip, especially who was dating whom and what all their friends were doing on the weekends. Laura learned to live vicariously, and she read novels voraciously. Much of her time, especially in the evenings after everyone else had gone to sleep, was spent imagining life after she got out of that itchy cast. She imagined herself running and riding her bike and going on dates and to school dances and ball games. She especially imagined taking a long, hot bath instead of having her mom give her a bed bath.

Ellie was just three years old when they brought Laura home from the hospital in her cast. Ellie thought the triangle bar on the chain above Laura's bed was neat-o! Ellie would climb up on the bed to sit beside Laura. She really wanted to sit on Laura's chest, but Mom got mad at her when she did. Ellie thought she should be allowed to do acrobats on that triangle bar, but she didn't, only because she had been barred from coming to see her beloved sister for a whole day when she tried it the first time. Laura loved it when Ellie came in to see her and then raced out to play with her dolls or her stuffed animals. She especially liked it when she overheard Ellie entertaining the Avon lady in the kitchen. Betty just shook her head and let her go, knowing Ellie irritated the daylights out of Mildred, an older spinster lady who came over once a month, but she didn't have the energy or much reason to try to stifle her exuberant youngest daughter.

Betty and everyone else in the family knew that they were spoiling Ellie, indulging her and always making her the center of attention. But they just couldn't help themselves. Every time Elmer or Betty tried to discipline her, one of her sisters rose up to her defense, so even if the punishment stuck, her sisters petted her and made her feel like she was very put upon for having to obey anyone's rules. Of course, they didn't have to punish her much or often because their notion of rules for proper little-girl behavior had relaxed significantly over the years. By the time Ellie came along, quite unexpectedly, both Elmer and Betty were far too busy and worn out to even notice behavior that would have shocked them when any of the others were that little. Ellie relished their attention and had no idea she was not the center of the whole universe.

Stella and Laura were in Laura's bedroom, waiting for the others to arrive. Stella was trying very hard for Laura's sake to act happy, but Laura knew she was beside herself with fear and worry for her mom. In just three weeks, Helen had gone from working full-time as a nurse to barely able to make it up the stairs to her bedroom in the evenings. The doctors were not giving them much hope that the treatments would work, and she was in terrible pain from the double mastectomy performed two weeks ago. Stella's dad was like a walking zombie, and both of her brothers were acting like nothing at all had happened, continuing to play sports and chase girls just as they had before the diagnosis. Stella wanted to strangle both of them, and even worse, she was angry, filled with rage all the time. How could this happen to her mother? Who did God think He was, putting her sweet mama through this nightmare?! Laura didn't have any answers for Stella, mainly because she wondered the same things. Laura wouldn't minimize Stella's grief and pain by giving her false hope or mouthing niceties about how it would all work out for the best. For now, they were looking absently through a stack of *Life* magazines.

In the living room, Betsy was setting the large dining room table that sat between the kitchen and the rest of the room. Grandma and Grandpa and Aunt Jessie would be there soon. Ten people would be seated around the table, a tight fit, but Betty had insisted that they all eat together on this special night. Elmer came in just before the rest of the family, and Betty let out a huge sigh of relief after he kissed her and went to their bedroom to take off his suit jacket and tie. Elmer's moods had evened out a little over the years, but she had seen him seething more and more earlier that week. She had been tense all day, waiting to find out if he was going to be in one of "those" moods tonight.

Right after Elmer left the kitchen, in came Jessie and the rest of them, and then it was just bedlam. Karen was taking jackets and hats, Betsy was taking dishes from the kitchen to the dining table, and Ellie was jumping up and down, getting hugs and talking nonstop to Aunt Jessie and everyone else about how she was learning to read and all about her new friends at school. Jessie's booming laugh filled the house, as did the smell of Grandma's cabbage rolls, which she brought to every family gathering. Betty thought they smelled like rotten eggs, but tradition was tradition.

When the food was all on the table and the tea glasses filled, Betty said, "Ellie, go get your sister and Stella for dinner. It's her birthday, after all." Ellie raced out of the living room to Laura's bedroom in the back of the house. When she got there, she stopped abruptly before going into the room. Stella and Laura were both lying on the bed on their stomachs with their bobby-socked feet in the air, looking a magazine, and laughing so hard they were crying.

Ellie said, "Hey, what's so funny?"

Laura and Stella looked up, still laughing, and they tried to catch their breath, but then they looked at each other and burst out laughing again. Ellie had no idea what was so funny, but she started laughing, too, slapping her leg and guffawing like Aunt Jessie.

From the living room at the other end of the house, it sounded like someone was in horrible pain, so Elmer ran back there first, then Betty, followed by all the others. To get to Laura's bedroom, they had to go through the hallway and the bedroom Betsy and Karen shared. Well, Betsy and Karen's bedroom wasn't very big to start out with, and they each had a bed and dresser, so there was very little room for all eight of them to see what was going on. Jessie was the last one in, and she tripped over a stepstool at the back edge of the room, falling into Grandpa, who tried to catch himself but pulled Grandma down as he went. Before anyone could figure out what in the heck was going on, Elmer looked back at the pile of his relatives on the floor, then back at the two teenagers in the other room laughing hysterically, and said, "Jimminee cricket, this nuthouse is going to kill me after all. You'd think there was a national crisis here. Now, get up and let's go have this blasted birthday party."

Betty, who was much too frazzled from getting ready for the party to put up with Elmer's crap, said, "That's all right. You girls just laugh all you want. I'm going to go put my feet up just as soon as I can get through this circus."

Ellie thought it was all just so grand. She fell down with a flourish, as if in a dramatic dying scene from some movie, pulling Karen down on top of her, and then Betsy dove on top of both of them. Elmer and Betty picked their way through the room as the older folks tried to help each other up, and Laura and Stella fell off the bed laughing harder than ever.

Eventually, they all made it back to the living room, took their seats at the dinner table, and stuffed themselves like royalty, with everyone talking the whole time. When everyone had finished their meal, Grandma and Karen got up and began clearing the dishes, and Betty brought the cake in from the kitchen. It was Laura's favorite, chocolate cake with vanilla icing— Grandmother Claxton's recipe. Betty had gone all-out and put seventeen candles on the cake. They lit all of the candles, placed the cake in front of Laura, and everyone joined in singing "Happy Birthday," off-key and loudly but with great gusto. Laura blew out her candles just as she wished for Stella's mom to get well.

As Jessie drove Fred and Annie home after the party, Fred shook his head, saying, "I don't like it one little bit. My Laura girl is torn up, and those two so-called parents of hers ain't doin' nothin' to take care of her. I'm telling you, Annie, I'm gonna go over there this week and tell that boy of yours to straighten up, or she'll be coming to live with us. That's all there is to it." Fred had fumed that way ever since they got back into Jessie's car.

"Fred, you know Laura will be just fine. It's nothing more than life throws at all of us. Her friend hurts, so of course she's sad, too. Now, hush!" said Annie. Everyone who knew Annie outside of her home thought nothing ever bothered her since she was always beaming, asking about everyone else, never complaining about her own life. But anyone who was around Fred and Annie for more than a half hour quickly found out that she never backed down from a fight with Fred, who gave her plenty of opportunities to do so.

"Okay. Simmer down, kids. Fred, don't fret. It only causes trouble," said Jessie, who had long since learned to tune out their bickering. "What we really need to do is make sure Annie has everything ready to pack for our trip. You know, we leave in just ten days, and I don't want any last-minute surprises."

"Yes, I have everything ready. I just have to do the washing and ironing the day before, so it'll all be nice and fresh. Do you think I need to pack my good blue suit in case we go somewhere fancy?" Annie asked Jessie.

"Sure, pack anything you like, just be sure it all fits in that one big bag."

Fred said, "I don't know what you women get out of all this rushing around the planet, risking your lives on an airplane to fly across the ocean, for God's sake."

Neither of them responded, having heard the same kinds of complaints every time they went anywhere. They both knew good and well that he loved having the house all to himself and that his complaints were just cover for his glee at the thought of beer, TV, ball games, and no woman fussing at him for two whole weeks.

They arrived in front of Fred and Annie's little house on Commercial Street, which was one block off South Main Street at the opposite end of Beacon from Elmer and Betty's house. Fred quickly said, "See ya, Jess," and got out of the car. Annie, still sitting in the back seat, stayed to talk to Jessie without Fred constantly interrupting. They discussed their plans for the trip for a while. Anticipating their next adventure was almost as much fun as the trip itself. Almost.

Jessie changed the subject after a few minutes, knowing that Annie was the only one she could talk to about what was happening with Betsy. "Annie, you know how concerned I've been about Betsy. Well, I'm afraid she's worse off than I first thought."

"No, that can't be," declared Annie, who wasn't blind to other people's faults, but who always looked for the good in them. As a result, Annie had taken up for Betty when Jessie first started telling her about how condemning and critical Betty had become with Betsy. "Surely this is just a little mother-daughter spat. We all act that way sometimes."

Jessie sighed and shook her head, uncharacteristically befuddled. "I wish it was just a phase, but I don't think so. Sure, Betty loves all those girls, but since little Ellie came along, Betty has really changed, especially toward Betsy. Why, the other morning, I went over there before the girls left for school. I made up a ruse that I needed to talk to Elmer before he went to the office, but I was there to check on Betsy. When I walked in, before Betty realized I was there, I heard her screaming at Betsy. It was awful. And worst of all, Betsy has stopped crying. Now she just stands there with a vacant look, as if she's not even there. And she's been so quiet when she comes to clean my office. I can't get a thing out of her, even when I have her quit cleaning to drink a soda with me."

Annie said, "Jess, you know how emotional girls are at that age. She's going to be thirteen soon, so who knows what's really going on inside her little head."

"That's true enough. But I don't think this is teenager stuff. I think this is something a lot deeper. Unless she finds someone with some sense to talk to about this, it's gonna sour her, for sure," Jessie said.

"You should talk to Betty about this. She'll surely lighten up if you do."

"Ha! That's a good one, Annie! No, I'm the last person she'd take kindly to hearing from that she's not doing her job right. Except Elmer, of course," Jessie told Annie.

Annie shook her head. *"Tch, tch, tch,"* she clicked with her tongue. Annie knew better than anyone else how headstrong her youngest son was. And she realized that his marriage to Betty was rocky on a good day. But she would have never thought that Betty would be downright mean to any of those girls. "Okay, we're going to pray about this. God will work it out just right. But in the meantime, we've got to do something to make it easier on my little sissy."

They sat silently for a bit, and then Annie said, "I'll call her before we leave on our trip and ask her to come stay with Fred a couple of nights. She adores him. If anyone can help, it'll be her grandpa," said Annie.

"There you go! That's just the ticket," exclaimed Jessie. "He may be a hardheaded old fool, but no one loves that little girl more than my brother. If he weren't such a grouch, I'd go in and give him a big hug right now."

Annie got out of the big Cadillac, and Jessie got out to give her the big blue enamel roasting pan that she'd brought the cabbage rolls in. As Jessie gave her the pan, she bent over and kissed Annie on the top of her white hair, and said, "Be sure not to tell Fred what's going on. He'd go over there and raise a ruckus for sure."

"Don't I know it," replied Annie. "He's got a heart as big as the heavens, but he never has had a lick of sense."

"Except the day he married you, Annie," laughed Jessie as she clambered back into her Caddie. The neighbor cattycornered across the street had been quietly observing them from his front porch. He chuckled when he saw the front of the car sag as if groaning under Jessie's weight. Jessie honked and waved her arm out of the window as she drove away.

Ten days later, in the middle of October, as the leaves on the maple and oak trees were beginning to turn red and gold, Betsy walked home from school. She hadn't stopped at Battles after school, even though all her best friends had gone. She carried a couple of books and a notebook for her weekend homework. Betsy knew the other kids liked her, and she was a cheerleader and did well in school. She loved her sisters, but she still felt so lonely. "Why don't Mom and Dad love me?" she wondered again. It was the never-ending unanswered question that had begun haunting her shortly after Ellie was born. Betsy loved Ellie, and she knew she was Ellie's favorite playmate. But she couldn't figure out why her mom had turned on her so viciously after Ellie was born. And she lived in fear of her distant father, whose mood swings ruled their lives.

At first, after her mom started railing on her, it was funny. She and Karen had made faces at each other and joked about it for the first couple of years. Then, it had gotten worse, until now Betsy was miserable almost all the time. The only time she got any relief was when she went to Grandma and Grandpa's house. Thank God she was going to stay with Grandpa for the weekend!

That thought lifted her spirits, so she started singing. "Everybody's doing a brand-new dance now, c'mon, baby do the loco-motion..." She moved down the sidewalk with a little bit of a bop in her step.

At home, Betty was getting ready for the Club ladies to come over that evening. She had banished Ellie outside for the afternoon, knowing she ought to be making her do a few little chores, but she didn't have the energy or desire to take the time to show her how to do things the right way. Ellie was outside, behind the house, digging a hole in the yard and talking away. She had a couple of troll doll families placed strategically around her. The trolls were cheering as Ellie, the bulldozer operator, dug the hole for their new community swimming pool. Ellie didn't realize Betsy would be home early today. Otherwise she would have been at the front corner of their lot, watching for her to come down the street. Ellie wasn't allowed to cross the street by herself yet. She planned to change that very soon.

As Betsy came around the corner to come in the back door of the house, she was still singing to herself, so she didn't notice Ellie sitting a couple of yards away from the back door, on the other side of the yard. Ellie was much too intent on her project to notice Betsy arrive at the stairs, but she turned to look when Betty opened the back door, flew down the steps, grabbed Betsy by the shoulders, and started shaking her, screaming, "You idiot! Why can't you ever do anything right?"

Betsy was shocked, dropped her books, and was struggling to free herself. Ellie shot up and ran to Betsy. She wedged herself between them and started kicking her mom in the shin, shouting, "Stop it! Stop it!" Betty lost her grip on Betsy when Ellie kicked her, and Betsy got free and ran inside the house, sobbing uncontrollably. Betsy locked herself inside the bathroom, the only room with a door that locked.

As soon as Betsy broke free, Ellie ran away through the back yards of the neighborhood, and Betty collapsed on the bottom step, with her head on her arms, crying in shame at her horrible behavior. She had known for a long time that she was out of control and abusing Betsy. Every night when she went to bed, she prayed that God would help her be better, more loving to Betsy. She loved all her daughters, including Betsy, but ever since Ellie was born, Betty became enraged almost every time she looked at Betsy. Today, as she was taking things for Club from the kitchen to the living room, she saw Betsy walking toward the house, bopping along, and before she knew what had happened, Betty was shaking Betsy like a rag doll and getting her shins kicked.

When Ellie was sure her mom wasn't running after her, she found a tree to hide behind. She saw her mom sitting on the back stoop, with her head on her arms, her shoulders heaving up and down. Ellie had heard her mom yell at Betsy plenty. Even though Betsy usually left for school crying, however, Ellie didn't think too much about it. She'd heard Mom talking to the other adults, and she always said nice things about all of them, including Betsy. Laura was the smart one, Karen was the nice one, and Betsy was the pretty one. Ellie figured she'd be all three. Ellie figured that Mom must be mad because Betsy was so pretty. She'd heard lots of old women like Mom talk about other women whom they called pretty, and they never sounded very happy about that.

Ellie decided Betty wasn't going back into the house soon, so she ran around to the front of the house and up the front porch steps. She raced through the house to try to find Betsy. Since she wasn't in her room, Ellie listened at the closed bathroom door. She could hear Betsy crying with the water running. Ellie knocked on the door and whispered, "Hey, Betsy. It's me, Ellie. Can I come in?"

"No, please don't, sweetie pie. I'll be okay. Just let me get my face washed," said Betsy. "Do you know Grandpa's phone number?"

"No, but Mom wrote it down in the back of the phone book. Why?"

"I want you to call him and tell him I'm ready to come over as soon as he can come and get me."

"Okay," Ellie agreed. She ran into the living room to the telephone table. She got out the phone book and turned to the back page. She found the name she remembered Karen had shown her, saying, "That's Grandpa's name, and that's his phone number. Now, promise me you'll call it if you ever need him or Grandma."

Ellie looked at the number on the page and picked up the telephone. She heard the dial tone and was glad Old Lady Parker was not on the line gabbing to her sister. Ellie had listened in once, and she couldn't believe old people could be so boring. Now, though, she was concentrating on dialing the right numbers, 5-4-7-3-4. After a couple of rings, she heard Grandpa's familiar, gruff voice yelling, "Hello! Who's there?!" Ellie held the phone out from her ear and said, "Hi, Grandpa. Can you come over now and pick up Betsy?"

"You betcha, little gal. How 'bout you come with her and stay with your old Grandpa, too?"

"No, Grandpa. It's Club night, and I've got to help Mom."

"Okay, I'll be there soon. You better come out and give me a hug before we leave, though," yelled Grandpa. Everybody said he thought he had to yell on the phone since his house was all the way across town.

Grandpa pulled up ten minutes later in his beloved, rusted-red 1940 Chevy truck named Lucy. Grandma had never learned to drive, which suited Grandpa just fine. He sure didn't want to share Lucy with no woman. Betsy heard Grandpa coming when he was a block away, and she ran out of the house with her little overnight bag, yelling, "Grandpa's here! I'm going."

Betty let her go without saying a word. She just stood at the sink washing dishes and trying not to feel like a total failure.

As Betsy drove away with Grandpa in his old truck, she instantly felt some of the weight of the world ease off her shoulders. She relaxed and turned on the crackly radio. As she turned the dial to her favorite radio station, she pushed her sadness a little deeper down and sighed. Maybe everything would work out all right after all, she thought hopefully.

10

Elmer took off work early on Thursday every week if possible. Normally, he went straight to the Elks to play poker and drink beer with his buddies. But today, he had decided to have some real fun. It was a week before Halloween, and all the kids were getting their costumes ready. Halloween was a big deal in the Lupeny household because Betsy had been born on Halloween, and eight years and one day later, along came Ellie. Elmer had had a busy, stressful week. Lots of tense negotiations hadn't gone as he'd hoped. Two of his best clients who were also good friends were adamant that he should change his strategy in a big case he knew he could win if they'd just get on board with him.

This afternoon, though, when he walked back from the courthouse after filing several pleadings, he couldn't help but feel mischievous. He'd always loved the autumn season, and today the sun was warm, the breeze was brisk, and his spirits were high. He drove home and then ran up the back stairs of the house, yelling, "Hey, Ellie, want to go for a ride?"

Ellie had been home from school for a while and was starting to get bored. It was not quite time for her sisters to get home from school, and none of her neighborhood friends, all boys, had come out to play since she'd gotten home. When she heard her dad yell for her, she dropped her book on the floor and ran to the back porch. "Yeah! I wanna go! I wanna go!" she cried as she hugged her daddy's legs.

"Okay! Betty, we're going for a drive," Elmer called down the basement stairs. Thursday was laundry day, and Betty had been hauling loads up and down the stairs all day. Tonight, she and Laura would be ironing, a task they both dreaded. Betsy had been relieved of all ironing duties after she had burned two of her sisters' best blouses. Karen, Laura, and Betty took turns, and this was Laura's week to iron while Betty fixed dinner.

When Ellie got in the car, she was delighted that her dad had the convertible top down on their old red and white Mercury. She squealed with delight when he whistled for Tubby, their 120-pound Saint Bernard, to get in the backseat. Ellie was the only one besides Elmer who could stand to ride in the car with the stinking beast. Tubby lived outside, as did almost all the neighborhood dogs and cats. The only bath he ever got was when Elmer took him to the pond at the farm where he kept his horses. He came out stinking worse from the foul pond water than before his bath. But worst of all, Tubby slobbered—epic drools of slime, usually mixed with dirt from laying his head on the ground. Everyone who came to visit them regularly knew to run for cover when Tubby shook his head; all that slobber went flying in all directions, sliming the skirts and faces and hair of those who were too slow to duck in time. Tubby loved riding in the car more than life itself. And riding with the top down was pure joy. Ellie turned around and scratched his head, telling him what fun they were going to have. Tubby rested his head on the back of the front seat, and neither Ellie nor Elmer paid any attention to the remnants of slobber left there when Tubby moved his head as they pulled out of the driveway.

Elmer drove toward the square but pulled over two blocks before they got there. He had a plan.

Betsy and Karen had met at Battles after school. They had to be home by 4 p.m., and Elmer knew they always began their walk home at three forty-five. The girls were walking with a couple of their friends from school who also lived on Maple Street. They talked and giggled as they walked out of the door at Battles. As they walked around the square, one of their friends said, "Hey, isn't that your dad?" She pointed toward a red and white Mercury convertible that looked like theirs—but they couldn't believe their eyes! Karen and Betsy almost dropped their books as they looked in horror—there was their dad and their little sister and their dog all wearing Halloween masks. Elmer and Ellie were waving their arms like lunatics, and Tubby was barking loudly and happily as they drove around the square. When Elmer was sure they'd seen him, he started honking the horn. Karen and Betsy were mortified! How could he? Didn't he have any sense of decorum at all!? Didn't he know that all their friends would see them?

They both wanted to run and hide, but by then, all the kids had run out of Battles to see what the commotion was about. Now their reputations were ruined forever. They would never forgive him! They couldn't believe it when their dad drove around the square, honking the horn with the dog barking for all the world to see a second and then a third time.

When they saw the car coming back around the square the second time, Betsy grabbed Karen's arm and tried to get her to run. But Karen just stood there, mouth open, looking like she was about to cry. Karen despised being the center of attention. Now, with all the kids laughing and pointing, she was not only the center of attention, but much worse, she was the butt of a terrible joke. How would she ever live this down?

Finally, Betsy got her attention, and they started walking, heads down and faces red from embarrassment. As the car passed them the third time, Ellie waved both arms and blew lavish kisses. Ellie felt just like a Hollywood movie star before a fancy ball. She knew her sisters would be as thrilled as her that their dad was so wonderfully fun.

After having so much fun riding around the square, Elmer decided to take Ellie and Tubby out to see the horses. He kept an old mare and the meanest pony that ever lived out at Jack Ward's horse farm west of town. Elmer wished he could spend more time there, and he couldn't resist taking Tubby and Ellie on this glorious afternoon. Elmer explained in his most serious, lecturing voice, "Now, Ellie, when we get out to the horse barn, watch out for Skyrocket. You remember the last time we were out there, don't you?"

Ellie said, "Yeah! Skyrocket nearly ran over me for no reason." She folded her arms and looked at him sideways to emphasize how mad that made her.

"I know, honey. He's very high-spirited. Just steer clear of him, and you'll be okay," Elmer assured her. He didn't tell her he'd beaten the pony with a whip after he had Jack take her inside the old farmhouse for a drink of water after it happened.

Ellie pulled her knees under her to sit up higher, telling him excitedly, "That's for sure. When you brought him home that day, he got loose from where you tied him, and Mommy had to go outside in her robe and house shoes to try to catch him." Ellie started laughing, and so did Elmer. Ellie could barely talk for laughing so hard as she recounted what happened after Betty finally got hold of Skyrocket's rope. "She held that rope, and Skyrocket galloped 'round and 'round in a circle until Mr. Winston came running out. Mommy would still be twirling in a circle screaming if he hadn't saved her!" she squealed through their laughter.

When Betsy and Karen got home, they were relieved that their dad and Ellie and Slobbergut, as they not-so-affectionately called Tubby, were not. They went into the house and immediately went to their room after yelling down the basement stairs at their mom. "We're home, Mom. Got homework to do."

Betty shook her head as she hauled another load of clothes to fold up the rickety, old basement stairs. How could five people possibly create this much laundry? She loved a neat and clean house, but laundry day was no fun whatsoever. As she brought the laundry to the dining room table to sort and fold, she heard her favorite song on the radio: "I Can't Stop Loving You," by Ray Charles. She had always wanted to have a great singing voice, but she knew hers was off-key and scratchy. She sang along anyway as she folded laundry. Laura would be home soon, and then Betty would let her take over the laundry so she could finish their dinner for tonight: beef stew with biscuits and apple dumplings with whipped cream for dessert. Betty knew no one else in the family cared, but she tried very hard every day to make their meals taste good and look nice.

She was relieved that Elmer had taken Ellie for a ride. That surely meant he would be in a good mood at supper. So often, he came home from work but wasn't really there. Something that bothered him about his day came with him and settled over him like a cloud. He never explained what was bothering him. Betty and the girls could only wait until he got furiously mad and started giving Betty a blistering with his hateful words, and sometimes with his fists. Until he blew up, he was silent. Totally. Sometimes they went for weeks waiting for him to say something, everyone walking on pins and needles trying to stay out of his way and not be the catalyst that set him off. The girls could go somewhere, stay with their friends or grandparents, but Betty had to stay.

She had thought of every possible option and reached a dead end every time. She couldn't divorce him. She had no money of her own, and none of the other lawyers in town were willing to go up against Elmer in his own divorce. She had nowhere else to go. All her friends were married with kids of their own. Her parents would let her stay with them, but her dad was not well, and their house far too little for her and all four girls. So, she stayed. But the strain of the lack of communication with Elmer and her outrageously confusing anger against Betsy was beginning to wear her out. She had no idea what to do. She just kept doing what she thought she was supposed to do, keeping her house clean and putting good meals on the table. Over and over and over again. The same every week.

Laura came in and told her that she'd start working on the laundry as soon as she put her books away. As the oldest, Laura realized more than the others that their mom was desperately unhappy and felt trapped. But she had no idea what to do to help, so she kept her thoughts to herself. She tried to help around the house as much as she could. The door to Karen and Betsy's bedroom was shut, so Laura knocked before she went in. They were sitting on Betsy's bed, but they stopped talking when Laura walked in.

"Hey, what's going on?" Laura asked.

"Oh, we're just ruined, that's all. Dad went too far this time," said Betsy as dramatically as she could.

"What now?" asked Laura as she walked through their room to hers.

"He rode around the square in that hideous convertible just as we were walking home, and he had the dog and Ellie and they were all wearing Halloween masks. Tubby was barking, and Dad was honking the horn. Ellie was screaming like a little monster! They went around the square like that *three* times! All the kids came out of Battles and laughed like it was just *so* funny." Betsy kept her chin and her indignation up high.

"Oh, my!" Laura exclaimed as she rolled her eyes. "You two should be used to his antics by now. And you know he'll just do something even worse if you complain about it. So, put on your big-girl panties and get your homework done before supper. I want you to do the dishes without complaining tonight. If you don't, I'm telling dad about Karen's little escapade with Tony."

Karen had been sitting on her bed with her back to Betsy and Laura, but she jerked around suddenly and said, "You wouldn't!"

Laura stared at Karen without saying a word, then turned and walked into her room. After she put her books down and took off her sweater, she came back through Betsy's and Karen's room without saying a word. Karen watched her intently, but in true Laura fashion, she didn't say a word.

At dinner, Betsy and Karen both stayed silent as Elmer and Ellie recounted their adventure in great exaggerated detail. Ellie couldn't wait to get to school the next day to tell her friend Suzy all about it.

After supper, Laura finished the ironing. Betty put away the clean laundry, and Betsy and Karen cleaned up the kitchen, this time without bickering. Ellie had gone back to "reading" the book she had dropped before her car ride. Elmer sat in his easy chair, watching the news and making notes on a yellow legal pad, as he did every evening after supper if he was home.

Suddenly, Ellie jumped up and said, "Auntie Jessie and Grandma will be back soon, won't they?"

Betty looked at Elmer, and he said, "Yes, I think they're supposed to be back tomorrow morning," thinking to himself that his respite from Jessie hadn't been nearly long enough.

Ellie yelled, "Yay! Let's throw them a big party with balloons and cake and ice cream and have all our friends come over to hear all about their trip." Ellie began twirling as if she were dancing, not concerned at all about the answer.

Betty rolled her eyes and sighed enormously. Elmer said, "Now you're cooking, little girl! That's a great idea. I'll call Dad right now."

"Now, wait just a minute, Elmer. I can't throw a party tomorrow. I've got to have some time to plan something like that," Betty told him. "Besides, we've already got plans next weekend to have cake and ice cream for Ellie and Betsy's birthdays."

"That settles it. We'll have the party then and celebrate everything at once," Elmer proclaimed, very pleased with himself for being so generous with Betty. "All we have to do is tell Jessie and Grandma, and the party will practically throw itself. I'll build a fire in the backyard, and we can have a wiener roast. All you'll have to do is buy some ice cream and hot dogs and have some drinks ready. Good thinking, Ellie!"

Elmer got up to go to the phone, and Betty shook her head, looking exasperated, a look all the girls saw too frequently. Betty thought, "He has no idea what he's asking me to do. I'll have to work all next week getting ready for this stupid party. Oh well, at least he's talking to us. Maybe he'll stay in a decent mood for a while."

The next morning, Fred was in the kitchen fixing his breakfast when he heard the front door open and Annie yelling, "Yoo-hoo! Fred, we're home!" He put down the toast he was buttering, shook his head, and yelled, "In here, old woman." He turned around to greet the world travelers. He couldn't believe his eyes. "Where in the world did you get all those packages?"

Jessie and Annie had come in the door carrying Annie's suitcase and several shopping bags each. Jessie boomed, "Well, good to see you too, brother. And yes, we had a fine trip, thanks for asking. Our flight was a little bumpy, but we got back safe and sound." She sat down Annie's suitcase and the packages, and so did Annie. Annie ran over to Fred, gave him a big hug, and said, "Oh, I missed you, Fred. But we had such a good time. I can't wait to tell you all about it."

Fred hugged Annie, glad she was back too, but he dreaded hearing about her trip. The first time through would be kind of interesting, but he knew she would tell and retell him every detail of their adventures over and over for weeks to come. Fred had no interest in traveling and almost no tolerance for female conversation. Still, it would be good to have Annie get back to cooking his meals again.

Jessie hugged Fred and made her way out of the house. She had to get back to her office to see if she still had any clients. She went straight to the office without going home first. She missed Goober, but she knew he'd be disappointed if she came home and didn't take him for a long hike right away. Leaving town for two weeks meant she'd have a mountain of work to plow through this weekend, and she had to assess the damage before jaunting off with her buddy. Good thing her friend Maudie didn't mind taking care of him for her.

Before going to the office, Jessie stopped at her favorite diner for a breakfast plate to go and a dozen doughnuts. As she walked up the stairs, Elmer was coming down with a stack of papers in his hands. "Howdy, nephew! How'd you make it here without me around to keep you in line?" Jessie joked, hoping to get a rise out of him. For once, Elmer didn't take the bait. He brushed past her quickly, saying, "Don't make any plans for next Friday night. Ellie wants you and the rest of the town to come over for a wiener roast. And save one of those doughnuts for me. I've got a new client you'll want to hear about," he called over his shoulder as he bounded out the front door in the direction of the courthouse.

Jessie topped the stairs and headed down the hallway with a giant, silly grin on her face. When she opened the door, she was surprised to see clients sitting in all four of the chairs to the side of Cookie's desk. "Well, hello, everyone, I just got in from Rome, so I hope nobody's got anything important for me to do. I'm not sure if I'm coming or going," she said cheerfully. "But here's some doughnuts to tide you over while Cookie and I catch up."

Jessie went into her office, and Cookie followed behind, closing the door. Cookie sat down in front of Jessie's desk and said, "Welcome back, boss lady. Those folks out there have a nasty will contest they want you to handle. It's perfect. The father passed away last week but made a new will last month leaving everything to his new, much younger wife. The kids are furious and out for blood. So, how was your trip?" Jessie pushed a pile of papers aside and sat down at her desk. She told Cookie the highlights of her trip as she tied into her breakfast of hot cakes, fried eggs, and a huge pile of bacon.

Jessie looked up from her food, wiped her mouth, and said, "Lawsy, I am so glad to be home where people actually know how to cook. You would not believe the lousy food they served us in Rome. Of course, Annie thought she'd died and gone to heaven. She got to go to the Vatican while I was working. She bought what she sincerely believes is the original pair of Jesus' sandals. I didn't have the heart to show her the hundred identical pairs at the market around the corner from our hotel," Jessie explained as she demolished her breakfast.

As she finished, Cookie got her up-to-date on the most important happenings during her absence. "Okay, now for the bad news," she told Jessie. "Jack found out that Tony Durham has been stealing motorcycle parts from Jay's Auto Repair. Tony has a buddy who works there who gave him a key. Jack is ready to go to the state's attorney with his evidence but wanted to wait to talk to you first. You know this is going to blow up, what with Karen mooning over that boy all over town and Tony's dad thinking he owns the whole county."

"Whooey!" Jessie exclaimed. "What a mess. I'll talk to Jack later today. Now. Let the show begin," she said, handing Cookie her dirty plate and following her out to bring in her new clients.

At the courthouse, Elmer was in the circuit clerk's office filing pleadings in several cases. He had a hearing in fifteen minutes and had to meet his client upstairs outside the courtroom. He joked with the ladies in the clerk's office, who knew he was full of bull but enjoyed his visits. Elmer knew how to make people laugh, and he was smart enough to realize that he got treated a lot better by these ladies when he used honey, not vinegar. Mainly, though, he was friendly with them because he felt much more comfortable with regular working folks than with most of the lawyers he knew. He'd grown up dirt-poor, and most of the other lawyers in the county looked down their noses at him. Plus, they dreaded having cases against him, knowing he would fight to the death over every possible issue. No detail was too small for Elmer to fight over it. His clients adored him because he fought so hard for them and didn't push them to pay him if they couldn't. When they couldn't pay him in cash, they brought him produce from their garden or butchered a hog or did odd jobs for him. In fact, Tubby was a payment from a client who raised Saint Bernards but who couldn't pay for Elmer to help him with a boundary line dispute.

This morning, Elmer was in a good mood because he knew he had a winner in court. He had filed a motion for summary judgment in a big personal injury case against his client, the owner of the largest grocery store in Beacon. A sweet old lady had slipped on a banana peel and had broken her hip. Elmer's motion could end the case in his client's favor if he could convince Judge Bigham that there were no disputed facts worth having a trial over. Elmer relished arguing in front of this judge because he had often ruled in Elmer's favor. But the real reason he felt so feisty this morning was that he knew his opponent, Dick Jerkins, was royally pissed off about the motion. Elmer had taken the depositions of all the major players in the lawsuit and had made them all admit facts that made Dick's lawsuit collapse in front of him. The men in Dick's family had all been lawyers for three generations back. Dick acted like Elmer had just walked out of a hog pen and was far too backward and uncouth for Dick to stoop to talk to. As a result, Elmer made sure he won every single case he could get against that pompous dimwit.

———

At the wiener roast, the Lupenys' backyard was filled with friends and family. There was a huge fire burning with bales of straw placed in a circle several feet back from the fire for people to sit on. Everyone had brought food for a potluck—baked beans, potato salad, deviled eggs, chips, dip, brownies, pies, and popcorn mixed with candy corn. Grandmother Claxton had made a cake that looked just like a cute blond girl in honor of her two blond granddaughters. She'd made one large round layer cake and two smaller ones. Then she'd used the large cake for the body, one of the small ones for the head, and she'd cut the other small cake into pieces for the hair. She decorated it all with colored icing. The cake was so special that the girls didn't mind a bit that they didn't each have their own birthday cake.

Laura sat back from the bales on a blanket with Stella. Neither of them talked much. The ashes rising from the flames held their attention as they tried to think about anything but how horrible life had become for Stella's mom. Karen and Betsy had been recruited to make sure all the guests knew where to put their food and get their drinks and hot dogs to roast. Ellie was in charge of keeping the little kids away from the fire. Laura and Stella would supervise any little kids who wanted to roast hot dogs or marshmallows.

Fred, Annie, and Jessie had arrived early. It was virtually a miracle that Fred had come at all. He hated big gatherings like this, far preferring to sit home watching TV in his comfy chair. But he knew that Betsy was having a hard time. He didn't know why, but he was worried about her and not willing to pass up a chance to make her laugh. Annie visited with everyone and helped Betty get everything organized. Jessie kept everyone entertained with her booming voice and tall tales. Everyone asked Annie and Jessie about their trip. Annie beamed as she exclaimed over the markets and people and the beauty and grandeur of the Vatican and the Sistine Chapel. Jessie beamed as she watched Annie tell and retell her stories. Jessie liked traveling well enough, but the best of it was seeing it all through Annie's eyes of childlike wonder.

Jessie looked over at Karen as she showed another guest where to put her food. Karen had a faraway look, and Jessie knew why. Jessie's heart hurt as she realized that Karen was about to experience her first real heartbreak. Jessie could still feel the crushing weight of losing the only man she'd ever loved. Jessie would have thrown herself in front of a train to save Karen or any of Elmer's girls, but she knew that Karen would be hurt much worse for much longer if she kept running with that hoodlum Tony.

Earlier that week, Jack had convinced Tony that joining the army was a much better option than facing a prison sentence. Karen would find out later that week that Tony was no longer living at home. He'd very prudently decided to go stay in Chicago with his uncle Hal while he waited for his military papers to come through. Jessie didn't care if he ever joined the military so long as he stayed away from Beacon.

Betty finally got a chance to sit down outside right after Elmer brought out the wieners and the sharpened sticks for roasting in the fire. Betty chatted with her friend, gratefully sipping an Irish coffee she'd made for herself before coming outside. Only the men drank at family gatherings like this, and only beer, never booze. But Betty had discovered that she was much better able to put on a good front for others if she had a little bottled encouragement. No one else but the girls knew how bad it was living with Elmer, and she wasn't about to change that.

Besides, after everyone left, she and the girls would have to clean up everything. And next week, she had to finish getting Ellie's Halloween costume ready. Ellie absolutely loved Halloween because she could dress up and go all over the neighborhood getting candy, and more importantly, attention. Although Karen and Betsy were much too old to go trick-or-treating themselves, they hadn't complained about taking Ellie around this year. Ellie was going as a cowgirl, and she didn't know yet that Betty's friend Flora had given her a horse costume she'd sewn years before for a play. Karen would put on the back of the horse, and Betsy would put on the front. Then Karen would bend over and hold on to Betsy from behind, turning the two of them into a horse. Betty laughed to herself, knowing that Ellie would have a fit of delight at having a "real" horse to trick-or-treat with her.

11

Karen stood at her locker hoping Marcia Belle Nolan wouldn't notice her. Marcia was the most popular girl in her class and the only daughter of Mayor Nolan and his snooty wife, Sara Belle. Karen despised Marcia, who thought it was her mission in life to spread vicious rumors about everyone not in her group of elites. Karen had to put up with Marcia in junior high because she was in all of Karen's classes and also played the flute in the band, but now that they were in high school, Karen planned to stay as far away from her as possible.

Karen rooted deeper into her locker, turning away from Marcia's clacking heels and swishing skirt coming toward her down the wide hallway. Karen had arrived early that Monday hoping to get to her home economics class before everyone else. As Karen gathered her books for class, Marcia made a beeline for her, saying loudly, "Toodles, Miss Karen, I am so glad I caught you. I just had to be the first person to tell you how awfully sorry I am for you, what with Tony leaving so suddenly and all."

Karen jerked her head at Marcia and asked, "What on earth are you talking about?"

"Well, darlin', you should know better than anyone that Tony Durham just up and left town with his bags packed this weekend. You know how close my mama and daddy are with the Durhams. Why, they practically live at our house when we're not at theirs or the club. But I'm sure you know much more about it than me, what with you running off to meet him every chance you get," said Marcia in her sappy Southern drawl. Karen wondered how she got away with acting like she had a Southern accent when she'd lived in Beacon all her life and should have had the same midwestern twang as the rest of the town.

Karen tried to hide her shock. She said, as boldly as she could, "Well, of course I know that. Now, excuse me, I've got to get to class." Karen felt her face flushing and her eyes beginning to tear up, so she busied herself with closing her locker. She fumbled with the bulky combination lock, not able to get the curved end of the lock through the holes on her locker door.

"Oh, you poor little thing, I can see you're simply devastated. But don't you worry a bit. Tony will write to you just as soon as he gets to boot camp. Isn't it just so dreamy that he up and joined the army like that? He'll be so handsome in his uniform. Why, he'll have to fight off the women coming after him more than he ever did here. Well, I won't keep you. I know how you always worry about getting to class on time. Toodle-oo," she sang as she swished away, a triumphant look on her perfectly made-up face.

Karen stood at her locker for several minutes trying to compose herself, fighting back hot tears of embarrassment. She had no idea that anyone besides Betsy and Laura knew about her seeing Tony. They had only been going out for a few weeks, but she thought he loved her as much as she loved him. After all, she had let him kiss her, and almost let him go all the way that one night. Surely, he wouldn't leave without even telling her good-bye. And what did that creep Marcia say about boot camp? Tony was joining the army?! None of it made any sense to her.

Finally, as other kids started filling the hallways, going to and from their lockers with loud chattering and laughter, Karen pulled herself away from her locker, leaving the door open and the lock in her hand as she walked in a daze to her classroom.

At home that morning, Betty was trying to get organized for Thanksgiving, which was only two and a half weeks away. She dreaded Thanksgiving more than anything. She sat at the dining room table with her cookbooks and a notepad. Every year, the whole family insisted on coming to her house for a huge turkey dinner with all the fixings. She had tried to get someone else to host it, but no one budged. It wouldn't have mattered anyway, because Elmer would have vetoed any plan to have the big feast elsewhere. "He has no idea what all I have to do to get ready for this extravaganza," she muttered to herself, and of course, she was right.

Thanksgiving in Beacon was not only the day for families to gather for an impossibly huge meal, it was also the homecoming football game between Beacon and its archrival, Westfort, and then the high school homecoming dance was that evening. Betty knew that only men could have come up with such a cockamamie idea. Why, either of those events required a mom of high school girls to plan and coordinate and buy outfits and get the girls' hair and makeup just right. And on Thanksgiving, of all days! There was food to buy and prepare, fancy dishes to be dragged out of cupboards and pantries, then washed and dried, and napkins and table linens to be ironed, and tables to be set. And that was just for the big meal at noon. Then she'd have to get everyone ready for the football game at 2 p.m., which Elmer insisted she and Ellie and Betsy attend, even though Betty didn't give a hoot about the game and would have greatly preferred to stay home. Of course, Karen and Laura would be going to the game. They were in high school.

Betty wished for the hundredth time that the ball game hadn't been made into such a big deal over the years, especially when the game was at home, which it was this year. The girls had already picked out their new outfits. Karen had a maroon tweed skirt and jacket that she'd wear with her black, patent-leather pumps. Laura had a black wool skirt and maroon plaid jacket that she'd wear with her new black heels. Thankfully, Elmer had a standing order at Dan's Flowers for the mums she and Karen and Laura would wear pinned to their jackets. It was an unbreakable tradition to wear a white mum adorned with a maroon B in honor of the Beacon Ranger football team. Oh, and then the girls would come home from the game and have just enough time to get their hair rearranged, reapply their makeup, and put their fancy dresses on before their dates arrived to pick them up, with Elmer recording it all on his 8mm camera, so they'd all have to watch it over and over. Betty's head was about to split open just thinking about it, and Betsy wasn't even in high school yet!

Betty went back to making her list of groceries to buy, using the menu she'd used for the last five years, grateful she at least had the meal planning down pat for now. She'd roast a big turkey, make a pan of her favorite dressing, as well as mashed potatoes, gravy, green beans, and cranberry sauce. She had to have Waldorf salad, everyone loved that. She'd placed an order at D'Angelo's Bakery for rolls and iced sugar cookies. Her mother, whom the girls called Grandmother, would bring her chocolate sheet cake. Aunt Ruth would bring pea salad even though no one else liked it. And Grandma Lupeny, of course, would bring her giant blue enamel roasting pan full of cabbage rolls. Betty could not fathom how anyone could eat those stinking things, but there were never any left over, and everyone raved about them. Why Annie insisted on putting sauerkraut on them was beyond her.

Betty finished her grocery list. She stopped to smoke a cigarette and then dry and put away the breakfast dishes before mopping the kitchen floor. She remembered her own high school years, long before she met Elmer, when she still had dreams of a happy marriage. Her family had been poor, but so was everyone else she knew. Betty was the oldest of three girls and the prettiest. Sure, her youngest sister, Laurie, was cute, but everyone told Betty how pretty she was. Betty acted like she didn't notice the boys staring at her or their whistles as she walked to town. Betty wanted to be independent, like the women she read about in magazines, the ones with careers and glamorous lives. She wanted to go to college, but she knew her father couldn't afford to send her, so she did her best to satisfy her longing for more by reading novels about other people's lives. She had been happy in high school even though she wasn't particularly popular or a good student. She realized now that it was easier to be happy when she could still dream about a better life.

Betsy waited at Battles for Karen that Monday afternoon, but she didn't show up. Finally Betsy said "so long" to her group of friends and started walking home by herself. She figured Karen had to stay at high school for something. She wished again that she was already in high school. Then she could always find a reason to stay after school in order to avoid her mother. Now she pulled her jacket tighter and faced into the chilly wind as she walked home, the dread of her mother's hatred far more painful than the biting wind.

She was grateful, however, that it was her night to clean Aunt Jessie's office. She hoped Jessie would be gone so Grandpa would come help her clean. Grandpa had never done a lick of cleaning at home, but he gladly did almost all the cleaning for Betsy if Aunt Jessie wasn't there. If she was, he'd act like he was there only to say howdy before heading over to the tavern.

Betsy was lost in her thoughts as she walked down Maple Street. She didn't notice Kenny Ingram, a seventh grader who lived a few blocks from her, ride up from behind her on his new Schwinn bike. Kenny had made a quick detour from his paper route when he spotted Betsy walking home. He pulled up from behind her and said, "Hey, good-lookin', whatcha got cookin'?" Betsy jumped and dropped her books, shooting Kenny an angry look. Kenny was smiling goofily with his black hair sticking out at every angle under his red Cardinals baseball cap and his bushy black eyebrows raised over his smiling, hopeful brown eyes.

"Oh, Kenny, you like to have scared me to death. Now, help me pick up these books," Betsy said, trying to sound mature and as if she didn't love Kenny's devoted attention.

Kenny jumped off his bike, letting it and the paper bag tied to the handlebars fall to the ground, the rolls of newspapers bound with rubber bands spilling out of the bag. He rushed over to Betsy, as grateful as a puppy to have a chance to be near her. As he gathered her books, he looked up at Betsy, whose arms were crossed in front of her and whose eyebrows were raised in a look she hoped conveyed disdain. "Hey, Betsy," he said with hope brimming in his eyes, "maybe you could come to my birthday party on Saturday. My mom is letting me invite as many kids as I want, and there'll be lots of eighth graders there."

Betsy took her time answering, knowing the wait would drive Kenny nuts. She finally accepted her books from him and said, "Well, thanks, but I'll have to let you know later. I may have other plans," she said, trying to sound mysterious. She started walking home, and Kenny began picking up newspapers, watching her all the way down the street until she turned off to go in the back door of her house.

As Betsy came through the door, Ellie was on the back porch going through her wooden toy box, searching for her Mickey Mouse ears. The show was coming on TV in a few minutes, and she had to find them. Ellie looked up as Betsy came in, then she dropped the lid and ran to hug Betsy. "Mickey Mouse is coming on. Hurry! I've got to find my ears!" Ellie exclaimed. Betsy put her books down, rummaged through the toy chest, and found the ears. Ellie squealed with delight, put them on, and raced toward the living room.

Betty was in the kitchen, the room next to the back porch. She listened to her two youngest daughters and marveled at how beautiful and carefree they both seemed and how easily they interacted with each other.

Betty vowed to herself for the hundredth time that she would not pick a fight with Betsy. As Betsy followed Ellie through the kitchen, Betty said, "Hello, honey. Did you have a nice day at school?" Betsy didn't look at her mom or stop walking as she said, "Yeah," and walked quickly through the kitchen. Betty's shoulders slumped as she watched Betsy walk away from her. Betty gritted her teeth but did not unleash the curses she wanted to hurl toward Betsy.

At supper that evening, Karen tried to act like she was eating, but she didn't fool her sisters. Laura had heard the whole story through the school's grapevine. Just as Marcia had intended, by second period the whole school knew about Tony leaving town suddenly to join the army without so much as a good-bye to Karen or any of the other girls he'd dated. Laura had told Betsy about it as soon as she got home. Ellie had finished watching Mickey Mouse by then and pretended that she was playing with her troll dolls in the corner of the room as she listened to their whispers.

Elmer was oblivious to the dramatic undercurrent, but Betty knew something was wrong with Karen. Although Betty didn't know that Karen had been seeing Tony, she knew her sad face came from a broken heart, a miserable state Betty had endured too often herself as a teenager. She tried to get Ellie talking about school to distract everyone.

Ellie was more than happy to tell everyone about her school day. "Boy, do I have news for you!" she exclaimed. "We're gonna have a Christmas program, and I'm gonna try out to be the band leader!" she said proudly. She chattered merrily about which kids she thought would play the triangles and which would play the tambourines. She was sure her friend Suzy would get to play a little horn, but she hoped that Murphy Jerkins wouldn't get to be the band director instead of her. "I just have to be the director. I've watched the choir director at church for years, and I know just how to do it," she said, waving her arms as if conducting a choir.

Karen said she had lots of homework to do and excused herself, grateful it wasn't her night to clean up after supper. As she was leaving the table, the phone rang and Betsy sprang up and ran over to it, nearly knocking Karen down. Karen hurried on to her bedroom, hoping no one could see that she'd begun to cry. Betsy answered the phone just as her parents had taught her, using her most grown-up voice: "Hello, Lupeny residence, Betsy speaking." After a few seconds, she took the receiver from her ear and yelled as loudly as she could, in decidedly less than a grown-up voice, "Karen, it's for you!" She waited for Karen to come to the phone, covered the mouthpiece, and then whispered, "It's Chuck Rice, you lucky dog!" As she and Laura washed and dried the dishes later, they whispered their hopes that Chuck was asking Karen to the homecoming dance. Maybe that would help her forget about that ratfink Tony.

Elmer gave Betsy a ride to the office on his way to the city council meeting. As the city attorney, Elmer had to attend all city council meetings, and tonight the budget for next year was on the agenda. Elmer had been trying to get receipts and an accounting for the mayor's pet project, the Widows and Orphans Fund, ever since he started the job two years ago, but the mayor always had some excuse. The city council members were all the mayor's cronies and never did anything but rubber stamp whatever he proposed. Elmer intended to get an accounting tonight, no matter what excuse the mayor came up with.

He and Betsy walked up the creaky wooden stairs and down the dimly lit hallway. Betsy turned left into Jessie's office, and Elmer walked a few more feet to turn right into his office, hoping, as always, to avoid Jessie. He cursed himself for forgetting his city file when he'd left the office earlier that day.

As soon as Betsy opened the door to Jessie's office, Jessie pushed back from her enormous desk and bounded out in her giant pink house shoes to catch Elmer. Jessie still had on the clothes she'd worn in court that day, her purple velvet skirt and gold satin blouse, but now the blouse was untucked, her jacket thrown over a chair, and her teased hair mussed beyond any recognition of a hairdo. She hugged Betsy on her way out, nearly crushing the poor girl, and said, "Hold on, sugar pie, I'll be right back."

Jessie tromped across the hall and into Elmer's office before he could get away. He winced as he turned around and said, "Can't talk now, Jessie. Gotta run or I'll be late." But Jessie more than filled the doorway, making Elmer's escape impossible until she decided to let him pass.

"Just hold your horses, Elmer Pie. We need to talk."

"Later, Jessie. I don't want to be late for the council meeting," he said as he feebly tried to push past her.

"You've got plenty of time, and you need to hear this. I have it on good authority that Mayor Nolen is up to something rotten with that Widows and Orphans Fund he manages. Now that you're the city attorney, you need to get an accounting for it." Jessie gave Elmer her most intense courtroom stare.

As much as Elmer hated to admit agreeing with Jessie about anything, he knew she was right about the mayor. Elmer had never trusted that weaselly coward. Elmer had served in the navy before the war and had signed up for the Army Air Corps on the day after Pearl Harbor. He knew Nolen was a draft dodger the first time he'd talked to him. Elmer prided himself in his ability to read people, a skill he understood was more essential to his law practice than all his book learning.

"Yes, Aunt Jessie, I know how to do my job," he said, more than a bit exasperated. "Now, please let me go."

Jessie stepped back to let Elmer leave, waving her hand toward the stairs. "Of course, you know how to do your job, dearie. Just don't forget who you work for, 'cause it sure ain't that self-serving mayor of ours."

Jessie went back into her office and called out to Betsy to come have a soda with her before she got started. Jessie went to the small break room behind Cookie's desk and got two bottles of Coke out of the little refrigerator, then sat down at the table. Betsy came in and said, "Thanks, Aunt Jessie, but I need to get to work soon. I've got to get home as soon as possible to finish studying for my history test tomorrow." Betsy had fibbed, just a bit. She had a test, but she never studied much since she got good grades anyway. The real reason she didn't want to stay long was that she thought Grandpa wasn't coming, and she didn't want to be alone with her aunt that long. She had felt Aunt Jessie's concern for her, and it made her uncomfortable. She didn't understand it, but she knew if she started talking about her mom, she'd break down. Instead of seeking someone to confide in, she'd decided the only way to survive was to stop thinking about it and act like everything was perfectly fine.

Jessie sensed Betsy would not respond well to any direct questions about her mom, so she took a more indirect route. "That's fine, darlin'. You only need to work as long as you can, never a minute more. But you might want to wait to have your grandpa take you home after he gets here."

As expected, Betsy visibly brightened when she heard that her grandpa was coming after all. "Oh, okay. I guess I don't need to leave real soon," she said, sitting down and accepting the cold soda. "Mmmm. I love cold Coke in a bottle," she offered.

Jessie said, "You got that right. Nothing like it." They chatted for a while about school and her friends. Betsy told Jessie about the party she was going to that weekend. Even though Kenny was just a seventh grader, Betsy had decided to go after calling her friend Debbie and finding out how many other eighth graders planned to go.

When her grandpa walked in, he said, "Howdy, gals. Got a sodie for an old man?" Betsy jumped up and ran to hug her beloved grandpa. Jessie got up and pulled another bottle of Coke out of the fridge. As soon as she opened it and handed it to Fred, she said, "By golly, I just realized I've got to run. I'm supposed to meet with Maudie tonight, and I'll be durned if I didn't almost forget. You two take your time and remember to lock up when you leave."

"We're not idiots, sister. Of course, we'll lock up. Now, git!" Fred complained loudly, giving Jessie a wink as she walked out the door.

Soon after, Grandpa dragged out the cleaning supplies and told Betsy to take the feather duster. He dragged out the mop and bucket and began filling the bucket with hot water for mopping the floors. He left the mop and bucket in the break room and took the broom into Cookie's office to begin sweeping. He'd rather die than do "women's" work at home, but here with his precious Betsy, he'd never been happier. He whistled as he swept, occasionally asking her if she was doing okay. Betsy couldn't help but smile as she dusted her heart out.

———

That Saturday, she felt more peaceful and happier than she had in weeks. Her mom hadn't let up on her at all, but she'd somehow begun to learn how to do what Grandpa said he always did when he had to deal with someone mean whom he couldn't get away from. "Betsy girl, I just pretend I'm a duck and let it roll right over me. If I don't let their meanness get inside, it rolls right back to them, and I can go on my merry way. Quack! Quack!" Betsy laughed out loud as she remembered her grandpa's words and how he always crossed his eyes when he said "quack." Before she left for the party, she hugged Ellie and even told her mom thanks for letting her stay overnight after the party at Debbie's.

At the party, Betsy had fun talking to her girlfriends about who was going with whom and what clubs they planned to join in high school. Just before they left, Kenny got up the courage to talk to her when she left her friends to use the bathroom. "Hey, Betsy, thanks for coming."

"You're welcome, Kenny. It was nice of you to invite me," she said, meaning it. Even though Kenny was much too young for her, Betsy couldn't help but like his puppy-dog sweetness.

That was all the encouragement he needed. "Please go to the movies with me next Saturday. I won two tickets for turning in the most money this month for the Widows and Orphans Fund. Elvis's new movie, *Girls! Girls! Girls!*, is playing," Kenny said eagerly, nearly running out of breath before he could get it all out. He'd practiced in the mirror all week, hoping not to mess up.

All the junior high kids went to the Saturday matinee at the Capitol Theater on the southeast corner of the square every chance they got. Mayor Nolen owned the theater and gave free tickets at no cost to himself as an incentive for the paper boys to ramp up their collection efforts for his fund. Elvis's new movie was all the buzz.

Betsy tried to let him down easily. "Oh, Kenny, that is so sweet, but I've already made plans to go with Debbie and Becky, so I can't go with you."

12

Jessie hurried across the Beacon Square, with the streetlamps reflecting their amber light off the thick powder of white snow covering the road as huge snowflakes drifted down around her. It was a Thursday evening in mid-December, and she had to get back to her office in time to catch Cookie. Jessie's trial was unexpectedly going into its third day tomorrow, so Cookie would have to reschedule everything else.

Jessie lumbered up the stairway to the sound of the wooden steps groaning under her weight. She had on her rubber galoshes over her black leather court pumps, and she sported a long, heavy red wool coat with white ermine collar, a gift to herself last Christmas after she won a huge settlement for the family of a client who'd been run over by a concrete mixer as he walked across the Beacon Square to pay his real estate taxes.

She was coming down the hallway just as Cookie and Jack were about to shut the office door. "Hold up there, kiddos. I need to talk to you both." Cookie smiled and shook her head, knowing what Jessie was about to tell her. She had already rescheduled all of Jessie's appointments as soon as her friend had called earlier that afternoon. Her friend Melinda was a court reporter and called Cookie any time she knew Jessie was going to be delayed.

Jessie followed Cookie and Jack back into her office. Cookie showed Jessie the appointment book changes as Jessie took off her coat and galoshes. "Gotta run now, boss lady. I've got to get supper fixed and get the twins ready for the Christmas program tonight," Cookie said as she left. Jessie reminded her that she'd be there too. The whole family was going to yet another school Christmas program because it was Ellie's first, and she'd been chosen to lead the band for her class's part of the program. Ellie had made each of them promise with a pinkie finger lock that they'd be there to watch her. How she loved an audience!

Jack stayed and followed Jessie into her office, where she took off her royal blue jacket and flipped off her pumps, sighing as she slid her tired feet into her beloved house shoes. "Good to see you, Jack. How'd it go in Arkansas?" she asked.

"Pretty good. I didn't think I'd catch you today. I was headed over to the Bocce to confirm some details with Gordie," Jack replied in his quiet voice. Jack was ruggedly handsome in a forgotten kind of way. The sort of man you never noticed until he was gone, but then you couldn't help wondering about.

"Great. Tell me the news."

"Well, ma'am," said Jack, "I don't have all the pieces yet, but it looks like our mayor has quite an operation going down there. He's telling everyone that his poor sainted mama and daddy left him a pile of money when they died and that he felt the good Lord leading him to come back to his old homeplace and give back, just like he's been doing here in Beacon. The folks I talked to seemed suspicious, given that Old Man Nolen was known to be nothing but a rich conman himself. But they don't expect anything else from rich folks."

Jack continued, "The 'little ol' huntin' lodge' Judge Terrance told you about is actually a big hotel Nolen is building. The word on the street is that he hopes to get gambling and liquor permits on top of hunting parties paying top dollar to come there to hunt. Truth is, they'll mostly be hunting fancy gals who'll be more than happy to accommodate for the right price. What I don't know yet is how he's funneling money out of the Widows and Orphans Fund. I'll have to get Maudie to help me with that."

"Yes, sirree Bob, now we're gettin' somewhere," Jessie exclaimed. "Good work, Jack. Get in touch with

Maudie, and let me know what you find," she said as Jack left. She stayed at her desk looking over the list Cookie had left her.

The Lincoln Elementary School gymnasium was filled to overflowing with the families waiting to see their children perform. The janitor, Calvin Dooley, who also drove a cab in the daytime and did maintenance and collected money at the drive-in during the summer, worked there at night to set up for and clean up after special events and ball games. He had set up two groups of twelve rows of metal folding chairs in front of the stage. Each class would walk between the rows before their performance.

Elmer and Betty got there early and were sitting in the front row with Ellie's sisters and Annie and Fred. They saved a seat at the end of the row for Jessie. Everyone wore their nicest Christmas outfits. Annie had crocheted little red and green carnations for each of the girls to wear pinned to their blouses. Betty hoped the program would start soon and move along quickly. She had already been to dozens of school programs over the years and could barely fake interest anymore. She was grateful that Ellie's enthusiasm allowed her to miss her mother's dread of yet another off-key but well-intentioned, overly long program sitting in uncomfortable chairs while she should be home getting everything ready for Christmas.

Elmer got up to go to the men's room and to check out the crowd. He always liked to know who was at the same functions as him in case he needed to schmooze someone or, even more importantly, if he saw anything he could file away for future reference. Elmer worked hard to know everyone in Beacon and Benjamin County. Every adult was a potential juror. Everything he knew about people could be used to better select a jury to give him the verdict he sought, especially since what he knew about one person was inevitably connected to something he knew about someone else. Living in a small community in a rural county made it easy to learn lots about lots of people. Jessie had demonstrated that in her career for decades, although Elmer thought he'd figured it out on his own.

As he walked down the middle aisle, he saw Judge Terrance and his wife, and next to him were Mayor Nolen and Sara Belle. Elmer stopped to greet them, remarking how nice they all looked. Cookie MacIntyre was just arriving, no doubt, Elmer thought, kept late working overtime for his aunt. Elmer waved to people as he walked out, recognizing almost everyone and hoping to talk to several potential clients at the meet-and-greet afterward.

In her classroom, Ellie danced around the room with her little conductor's baton. She was wearing a bright red velvet empire-waist dress with white tights and her brand-new black patent leather shoes. She twirled so that her dress fluffed out around her. She couldn't wait for her family to see how well she remembered when to have each band member play their instruments. Suzy watched Ellie and shook her head a little but smiled. Ellie was so full of herself, but Suzy couldn't help but be excited too, even though getting on stage in front of everyone seemed more like a punishment than a reward to her.

Mrs. White clapped her hands and told them to line up in order. "Children, it's time for us to march down to the gym and take the stage for your big performance. Now, let me look you all over. Jimmy, remove that bucket from your head, or I'll have you sit with your parents. Everyone, show me your instruments." Everyone raised their little instruments in the air. There were triangles, horns, tambourines, and jingle bells. Ellie stood at the end of the line with her little baton. They were going to play one chorus of "Away in a Manger" and end with "Jingle Bells," and Ellie was to stand in front of the whole class. The others would face the audience in a semicircle, and Ellie would have her back to the audience. Mrs. White had the two biggest boys, Murphy Jerkins and Brian Bowers, stand in the middle so their parents could see them over Ellie, the littlest one in the class.

As they marched down the hallway, Mrs. White stopped them before they got to the gym. As the first act, she had to listen for the principal to announce them. Just as Mrs. White was telling them it was time to go, Ellie realized that she had to go to the bathroom—badly. She held up her hand, and Mrs. White said, "Not now, Ellie. You can tell me after our performance," and she began marching ahead of the children, who all followed in line behind her.

Ellie knew there was no time to go. She'd miss her big performance if she went now, so she'd just have to hold it. She breathed in a large breath and ran to catch up with them just as the last student before her entered the gym. She proudly walked behind the class, looking at everyone looking at her and smiling from ear to ear. Mrs. White climbed the stairs to the stage and watched as each child took their assigned place. Ellie walked in front of the class and curtsied dramatically before turning around to face her band.

Ellie did not realize it would take Mrs. White so long to go back down the steps and get seated at the piano.

Ellie kept looking over her shoulder toward her teacher, who was taking forever to get her music arranged and play the first note, which told the children to start playing. While she waited, Ellie crossed her legs and tried very hard not to dance around too much.

Finally, the first song started, and Ellie pointed to each set of instruments at the right time for them to do their part, all the while squirming more and more as she tried to hold it in. They got to the end of "Away in a Manger" and had just begun "Jingle Bells" when she couldn't hold it anymore, and so she peed right there on the stage and kept conducting. The two big boys in the middle noticed first and started laughing and pointing at her, then Mrs. White looked up from the piano and hit a loud, very sour note when she realized what had just happened. She nearly fell off her stool trying to get up and onto the stage before the whole crowd noticed.

But everyone noticed—most especially Ellie's family. Elmer's face got red, then purple, as he watched in horror and listened to the crowd trying not to laugh but erupting in huge guffaws and howls all around him. Betty just sat there with her mouth open and hands folded in her lap, thinking she would surely die of shame, a sentiment shared a hundredfold by Ellie's sisters. Grandma and Grandpa and Jessie just laughed along with everyone else as Mrs. White hastily ushered the children off the stage and out of the gym. Elmer, too embarrassed and angry to sit still, quickly walked out the side door with his head held high.

The crowd finally settled down, and the lady sitting behind Betty, Carol Jerkins, Dick's wife and Murphy's mother, tapped Betty on the shoulder. When Betty finally turned around, Carol whispered, "It's okay, honey. Everyone will forget all about this by next week." Elmer and Betty were not part of the Jerkinses' elite crowd, and Betty recognized Carol's condescending tone, having heard it from uppity women all her life. Betty and Ellie's sisters all knew that no one would ever forget this fiasco.

Just as Betty turned back around, she heard a loud squeaking sound coming from the back of the gym. Betty and everyone else turned around to see Mr. Dooley dragging a large mop and water bucket across the gym floor. He was a tall, lanky fellow, gaunt of face with his clothes hanging loosely from his skinny shoulders. He smiled a little but otherwise didn't look at anyone as he made his way to the front and then dragged the large, sloshing bucket up the five steps to the stage. By this time, Karen had her face in her hands, trying to stop seesawing between laughing and crying, horrified that she was calling attention to herself. Betsy and Laura just sat frozen, thinking they'd probably fall out of their seats if they moved a muscle. The crowd began laughing again in little pockets here and there. Every time the girls thought it was over, someone else started laughing again, setting off the whole crowd.

When Mr. Dooley finally got the bucket on stage, he wheeled it to the center and lifted out the giant string mop, sloshing water all over the stage, taking his time to mop the whole area and then wring out the mop to begin all over again. The whole process took only a couple of minutes, but Mr. Dooley relished thinking about how grand it would be when he told Earnest and the rest of his buddies this story.

Elmer never came back, knowing Jessie would load everyone into her Cadillac when the program was over. When the principal finally announced that they would take a short break to let the floor dry before resuming the performances, Betty commandeered Jessie to get everyone out to the car "right now" while she went to retrieve Ellie.

Back in the classroom, Suzy told Ellie not to worry about the other kids laughing at her. Suzy thought Ellie would be as embarrassed for herself as Suzy was for her. But Ellie hadn't realized until that moment that everyone had been laughing at her. She had thought they were just laughing because it was funny. She told Suzy, "I had to go so I went. What's the big deal?" Then she looked at Mrs. White, who was seated at her desk holding her head in her hands. Ellie's mom came in, lips pursed tight, and without a word, had Ellie put on her coat and whisked her out the door.

Ellie had the glimmer of a thought that this might be a bigger deal than she had figured. She did not realize it would only be the first of hundreds of "most embarrassing" moments to come.

13

For once, Betty didn't dread going to church. It was Palm Sunday, and she didn't have to cook a single meal for anyone. Laura had spent the night at Stella's. Helen had lost her battle with cancer three weeks earlier, and Laura was staying over there as much as she could to help Stella with the cooking and cleaning for her dad and brothers. Betty couldn't believe Helen was really gone. But Helen had suffered so terribly that Betty felt more gratitude that Helen's suffering was over than grief for her loss.

Early that morning, Elmer had gone to D'Angelo's Bakery for a dozen doughnuts for their breakfast. All she had to do today was set out the milk and make coffee. What a luxury! And that afternoon she could finish her book in peace and quiet after they all went to Two Tony's in Westfort for their all-you-can-eat buffet. Everyone but Jessie was going to church this morning to hear Betsy sing a solo. Betty marveled that she'd been able to listen to Betsy practicing all week without tying into her once. Betty had no idea why the rage had subsided, but she anxiously hoped it was gone for good.

As Betsy and Karen got ready for church, Karen told Betsy about the fun she'd had with her friends the night before. Karen's good friend, Kathy Baker, who lived a block away, had had a slumber party for her sixteenth birthday. All of Karen's best girlfriends were there, and a bunch of boys had come over to eat Sloppy Joes and have birthday cake with the girls. Of course, Kathy's mom had ushered all the boys out long before any hankie-pankie could happen. Karen confided in Betsy, "I think I like Chuck after all."

Betsy said, "It's about time! He's only been trying to get you to go out with him since September," as she pulled her church dress over her head.

Karen said, "I know. I just couldn't get Tony out of my mind till now." Karen had finally been able to come out of her funk a few weeks ago, when she'd started talking to the girl sitting next to her in typing class. Karen had known Molly Pavlis since junior high but had never talked to her before. Karen knew she was poor because of the way she dressed. She'd never paid any attention to Molly before, but this year, she'd begun to notice that Molly almost never talked to anyone. She looked down as she walked through the hallways alone. Her hair was almost always greasy, her shoes had holes, and her eyes were hollow.

Karen, drawn to Molly's loneliness, had started talking to Molly when the teacher was out of the room. Molly had seemed so grateful that Karen had invited her to sit with her at lunch one day. Karen began sharing her lunch with Molly. "Oh, please help me eat some of this. My mom always packs way too much for me," she told Molly. Karen knew that Molly wasn't fooled, but she was pretty sure that Molly was glad for both the food and a way to avoid any hint of sympathy from Karen.

It turned out that Molly was one of Earnest Pavlis's kids. Karen wasn't sure how many siblings Molly had, but she knew there were a bunch of Pavlis kids. They lived out south of town on an old, run-down farm. When Karen had mentioned her new friend at supper one night, her mom told her that Molly's mom had been in and out of the hospital a bunch of times over the past year. Betty knew the family because Elmer had represented Mr. Pavlis a while back.

As she talked to Molly at lunch most days, Karen came to realize that she wasn't as sad about losing Tony now that she had someone she could help. Karen liked trying to get Molly to open up and talk about her life without prodding her or making her uncomfortable. Molly often said, "Oh, Karen, you have no idea how nice it is to talk to you." In just a few weeks, Karen had seen a spark of light come into Molly's shadowed eyes. She still had holes in her shoes and wore pathetically old, outdated clothes, but her hair was clean, and she even smiled sometimes. Karen loved seeing Molly transform from an empty shell into the sweet, kind, smart girl she was meant to be.

Karen didn't explain any of this to Betsy because she barely understood it herself. Betsy was just happy that Karen wasn't crying over that louse Tony any longer. She asked Karen if her dress looked okay. Karen said, "You look so pretty, Betsy." It was true that Betsy was still a skinny thirteen-year-old, all elbows and legs, but she was blossoming into a real beauty, especially when she let her naturally funny and compassionate personality shine through.

Elmer knocked on their door and said, "Get a move on, girls! We're burning daylight!" He hadn't said much, but he was bursting at the seams with pride over his little girl singing a solo today. Before the girls could respond or even open the door, Ellie burst through. She had her Sunday dress and shoes on, but her hair was a mess. Karen grabbed her and said, "Not so fast, you little heathen. I've got to fix your hair." Ellie squealed and tried to get away, but Karen held her arms tight as Betsy grabbed her feet. They carried her that way, swinging her from side to side as she continued to squeal with laughter, and they maneuvered through the hallway to the dining room table, where Betty had already set out the brush, bobby pins, and ribbon. They plopped Ellie into the seat, and Karen got busy taming Ellie's wild hair. This was Ellie's most dreaded part of getting ready. She knew if she didn't sit perfectly still, which she considered pure torture, Karen would "accidentally" gauge her head with a bobby pin. Betty had insisted that Ellie's hair be put up in a bun on top of her head so that it would stand a chance of staying put, at least until they got out of church.

At church, the whole family sat in the third pew from the front, on the far right of the sanctuary. Betty had insisted years ago that they sit close to a door for easy escape with unruly children or a crying baby Ellie. When they arrived on this day, Grandma and Grandpa were already there waiting. Grandma regularly attended the Catholic church but gladly chose to come to the Baptist church today to hear Betsy sing. She was thrilled to have Grandpa with her. He had never attended the Catholic church with her, but he could be enticed from time to time to come see his granddaughters perform here.

After the announcements, the congregation sang a few hymns. Then the choir sang "The Old Rugged

Cross." Betty held back tears as they sang, feeling overwhelmed. The hymn was her mother's favorite, and it always reminded Betty of her precious childhood. Her mom had often been distant and sometimes cruel in her words to Betty, but over the years, Betty had begun to see how the struggles her mom faced had been the source of much of her bad behavior. She was beginning to see how much her mother had always loved her and done her best. That Betty had suffered now seemed of little consequence compared to her mother's love. Maybe that was part of what the preacher was always harping about in his sermons, those Betty had paid any attention to, anyway.

After the choir finished, the choir leader motioned for Betsy to come up to the platform. Betsy squeezed Karen's hand as she got up. She walked up the two steps and stood behind the large wooden podium, barely clearing the top with her head. She adjusted the microphone, but Elmer knew it wouldn't be necessary. "My little girl can sure belt out the songs," he thought proudly. When Betsy nodded at the pianist, she nodded back and began playing the first chords of "Softly and Tenderly." Betsy began signing softly, but then her voice rang out clear and strong as she sang the words that had come to mean so much to her: "Softly and tenderly Jesus is calling, calling for you and for me. See on the portal's He's waiting and watching, watching for you and for me. Come home, come home, ye who are weary come home. Earnestly, tenderly Jesus is calling, calling, O sinner, come home."

Betsy felt like she was soaring along with her voice. She'd always loved to sing, but this time was completely different. She felt an unexplainable joy and a release.

Betty felt something, too, but holding back her tears had tied her up in knots. Instead of release, Betty felt panic as she could no longer hold back the flood of tears and tangled emotions behind them. She knew if she stayed in that sanctuary a minute longer, she'd lose her mind. She got up quickly and tried to get out of the pew without being noticed, but she had to step over too many people to get out unnoticed. As she made her way out, tears streamed down her face.

On the final chorus, Betsy finally caught sight of her mom leaving. Seeing her brought Betsy back to earth. She assumed her mom was leaving because she hated her singing.

Nothing could be further from the truth. Betty thought her beautiful daughter's singing was far sweeter and closer to God than any angel's voice could ever be. Betty just had no idea how to deal with the flood of whatever she was feeling. She ran down the steps outside the sanctuary and all the way to the bathroom in the basement. There, she covered her face with her hands, fell to her knees, and sobbed her heart out for several minutes. She had no words to express or understand what was happening. Eventually, she got control of herself, blew her nose, splashed water on her face, and tried to compose herself enough to return to the sanctuary. As she climbed the steps again, she could only pray, "Help me, Lord." She had no idea of how willing and able He was to do just that.

When she got back, the preacher was already speaking, and she made her way back over to her family, gently touching Betsy's cheek and looking her in the eyes as she passed her. "You sang beautifully, honey." Betsy wanted to believe what her mom said, but she wasn't ready to trust her yet.

Betty couldn't make any sense out of the rest of the preacher's message, but one statement pierced her like an arrow: "If I do not wash you, you have no part in Me." For some reason, Betty remembered those words and the scripture they came from—John 13:8—and she couldn't get them out of her head for the rest of the day.

After church, the family and many others congratulated Betsy on their way out to the car. Betsy was amazed by their response, but she was even more amazed by her mom's deep hug and apology for having to leave during her song. She was sure her mom had never apologized about anything before.

At Two Tony's, the family trooped in and found a table large enough to accommodate them all. After everyone ordered their drinks, they went through the buffet line and piled their plates high with fried chicken and catfish, mashed potatoes, gravy, green beans, hush puppies, and dumplings. Grandpa was last to get back to the table, and everyone looked at his plate as he gingerly put it down. "Wow, Grandpa! I didn't know one plate could hold so much food," Ellie cried in amazement. Truly, Grandpa could have won a plate-piling contest if there'd been such a thing. "What are you all looking at? I plan to get my money's worth here," he explained as he grabbed his napkin and fork.

"Slow down, Dad," Grandma said. "We've got to say grace over this wonderful meal and blessed day first. Elmer, please say grace, would you?"

Elmer didn't like being put on the spot or praying publicly, but he accepted his mom's request. Everyone bowed their heads as Elmer quietly prayed, "Dear Father, thank You for this fine day and for allowing us to be together. Thank You for this most excellent daily bread. Amen."

Everyone dug in and talked over each other as they devoured the food. Ellie asked Grandma where Jessie was. Grandma told Ellie, "She went down south to a place called New Orleans, honey. She goes there every year around this time to catch up with an old friend and march in the Easter parade."

"Oh boy!" Ellie exclaimed. "I wish we had an Easter parade here."

Grandpa chimed in, "Your aunt Jessie fits right in down there, little darlin'. She always says she feels more at home there with the other weirdos than anywhere else."

"You got that right, Pop," said Elmer.

At home that afternoon, Betsy and Karen stayed in their room with the door shut so they could listen to the radio. Ellie played with her troll dolls in the living room as Elmer played a Pete Fountain record. After a while, he got out his clarinet and played along to a couple of the songs. Ellie asked him the name of the last song he played. He told her, "Stranger on the Shore." Ellie loved it when her dad played this record. Something about it made her feel closer to him than anything else.

Betty had gone straight to her bedroom after they got home. After taking off her good clothes, she put on her favorite comfy slacks and sweater, fluffed the pillows just right, and sat on the bed. She picked up her novel and opened it at the bookmark, but she didn't start reading. Instead, she pondered for quite a while over what had happened at church. As the music from the girls' radio drifted quietly through their closed door, it competed for her attention with the Dixie melody coming from Elmer's clarinet. Somehow both tunes united into one harmony. Betty put down her novel and reached into her nightstand. She pulled out her old Bible and turned the pages until she found John 13.

14

Maudie and Jessie sat at a table in the front window of Ingert's Café, their favorite diner. It was a gorgeous day in early June. The sun was shining through the plate glass as dust particles floated on the sunbeams. They had staked out their spot just after 12:30 p.m. on that Friday afternoon, knowing they could see directly across the Beacon Square to the front steps of the courthouse where the action would begin shortly.

As they chatted quietly, drinking iced tea and finishing their pie, they watched people go in and out of the courthouse and cars travel around the square. They finally spotted one of the cars they were looking for. It was a brand-new shiny black 1963 Cadillac. It pulled up to the front of the courthouse, and Mayor Nolan hopped out and stepped over to the passenger door. He opened it, and out cascaded Sara Belle in her finest First Lady getup, a lilac satin suit with a lilac hat placed just so over her bleached blond and perfectly teased coif. Lilac pumps and a purse completed the ensemble.

The mayor had learned long ago to cater magnificently to Sara Belle. "Right this way, my dear. The press will be here shortly," he said as he escorted her up the steps and into the courthouse.

Jessie shook her head as they watched them. "Whooee! I'd give a boatload of money to find out what kind of story that little worm fed Sara Belle so she wouldn't find out the truth."

Maudie shook her head and laughed quietly. "I don't want to know the first thing about what those two talk about. I'd be sick for a week." Jessie laughed, then said, "Oh, look! There's Joe!" The long time state's attorney, Joe Harley, pulled up in his Pontiac convertible, top down. He unfolded his long, angular frame, straightened his light blue seersucker suit, and walked quickly up to the courthouse.

Maudie sighed loudly and whispered to Jessie, "I thought I'd have a heart attack until you flipped that crook." Jessie laughed but agreed that it had been touch and go for a while. "Good thing I found out about his little affair with Sara Belle, or we wouldn't have been able to pull off any of this," she whispered back.

After Christmas, Jessie had been meeting a client in a neighboring town when she happened to run into Joe and Sara Belle coming out of her client's motel at six o'clock on a Saturday morning. Jessie had gone right up to them and invited them to breakfast. Well, she didn't exactly *invite* them. It was more like she had barreled out of her car, strode up to them in her impossibly huge, red buffalo check jacket and favorite bright purple felt hat with its jaunty peacock feather, put her arms around them, and escorted them into the Hungry Jack restaurant, exclaiming the virtues of the pancakes and eggs to which she planned to treat them.

Sara Belle had flushed and sputtered, but she could not get out of Jessie's bear-sized hold. Joe allowed Jessie to escort them, trying to think of some scheme to get out of his mess, but he was unable to recover from the fog of last night's whiskey. She ushered them to a center table and explained to them what was going to happen, in between ordering everything on the menu. "Sara Belle, I do declare you've never looked younger or prettier. Now, eat up, honey, you're gonna need your strength," she said with the same gusto as when she gave her closing arguments before juries.

Joe sat pale and silent as Jessie explained her plan. Sara Belle would go home to her husband as if nothing had happened, which would be all too easy for her, since he was used to her overnight "shopping" trips with her girlfriends. They both knew she wasn't shopping, but they had long since effectively separated, living in the same house but neither having anything to do with the other except for the mayor's official functions and Sara Belle's endless parties. Sara Belle wanted to live in a fine home, wear fine clothes and furs, and see her picture in the papers regularly. The mayor just wanted to get out of Beacon with as much money as he could.

Jessie explained in painful detail that Joe would meet with Jessie the next week to go over her list of criminal clients. He would find deals for each of them that would make everyone happy. Joe was more than happy to oblige her, but he did not know that Jessie's clients were just the first part of the deal she would make with him. When their meeting was over, Jessie had secured a solid deal that would have the mayor paying back every cent of the money he had stolen from the Widows and Orphans Fund, with interest, in order to avoid both state and federal criminal charges. Of course, Jessie threw in a sweet, off the books deal for her client who had originally tipped her off about the mayor's poker games.

Jessie had made a believer out of Joe by showing him photographs of him and the mayor going in and out of the little hunting "shack" in Arkansas. The "shack" had turned out to be a four-thousand-square-foot, five-bedroom mansion just outside Hot Springs, with a dozen of the cutest little cottages you ever saw on twenty-five acres of prime hunting grounds. It seemed that the mayor had developed an exclusive hunting and gentle-men's club on the property. Not only could his bigwig buddies hunt deer and turkey there, but they also could choose from a dozen young girls for their pleasure after the hunting was over. No wonder the mayor was so in-terested in the young girls from Benjamin County who had run away from home over the years. After seeing Jessie's evidence, Joe had easily convinced Mayor Nolen to go along with the deal.

Maudie and Jessie watched out the café window as the local news stations and reporters showed up along with a large crowd of curious townspeople. Everyone knew the mayor was going to make a big announce-ment at one thirty. Maudie had been in charge of the publicity. She had dropped hints with all the newspa-permen she knew, and she and Jessie had written a juicy article they had Joe sign. State's Attorney Harley teased the readers with hints about his big announce-ment to be made on the courthouse steps.

With the people gathered and the cameras rolling, Joe, and then the mayor and his adoring wife came out of the courthouse doors, looking as humble and pious as they could. When all the attention was riveted on them, Joe stepped forward and began.

"Ladies and gentlemen, it is my distinct pleasure and honor to announce to you that I am resigning, effective today, as Benjamin County's state's attorney."

When he was sure the crowd was sufficiently bowled over, he explained that he had always wanted to sail all over the Bahamas, so he had invested in a small sailboat and planned to spend his golden years in the salty sea air. He then turned to Mayor Nolen, who told the crowd that he, too, was retiring, realizing that he had done all he could for the great town of Beacon. He hoped the town would carry on the fine traditions he had started, but he was going to spend the rest of his days helping the needy people of his and Sara Belle's home state, Arkansas. At this, Sara Belle let out an audible groan, but she quickly covered it up with a loud cough and the most adoring look she could muster at her insipid husband.

Jessie and Maudie watched the announcement. They could hear enough of the speeches to be sure those scoundrels were being faithful to the preplanned script. Besides, Jessie had the whole portfolio of the evidence of their crimes next to her in her briefcase, including all the receipts Maudie had gathered from the newspaper and banks showing the ridiculous amounts of money paid to the Widows and Orphans Fund over the past fifteen years. Maudie had obtained the information easily when she had explained that the mayor was being considered for a national award honoring the mayors of each state who had done the most good for their respective communities. Jessie had just as easily convinced the mayor to turn over his own records of the paltry sums of money paid to the widows and orphans. He was not so stupid or reckless to think he'd have better luck staying out of trouble if Jessie simply turned all her information over to the FBI.

Jessie and Maudie knew all three of those rats would slink away, believing that saving their reputations was all that mattered. Jessie was mighty disappointed that she didn't get to drag them through the local mud just a little, but Maudie was as content with the outcome as her big ol' fat cat. She and Jack had both put the word out with their contacts in Arkansas that anyone who cared about holding on to their money should watch out for Mitchell Nolen. And earlier that morning, Jessie had told her about the next case she'd be working on. Maudie was already planning just how to crack it.

CPSIA information can be obtained
at www.ICGtesting.com
Printed in the USA
LVHW021047020920
664820LV00011B/883